THE RELATIONSHIP DEPOT

Building Relationships That Last A Lifetime

2nd Edition

Jeremy Mahood

Copyright © 2011, 2018 Jeremy M. Mahood, PhD
All rights reserved. No part of this publication may be reproduced, stored in a retrieval system, or transmitted in any form or by any means – electronic, mechanical, photocopy, recording, or any other – except for brief quotations in printed reviews, without the prior permission of the author.

Library and Archives Canada Cataloguing in Publication
Mahood, Jeremy, 1950-, author
The relationship depot : building relationships that last a lifetime / Jeremy Mahood. -- 2nd edition.
1. Marriage--Religious aspects--Christianity. 2. Spouses--Religious life. I. Title.

BV4596.M3M34 2018   248.8'44   C2018-902776-2
                                    C2018-902777-0

Issued in print and electronic formats.
ISBN 978-1-988989-02-0 (softcover).--ISBN 978-1-988989-03-7 (PDF)

All scripture quotations, unless otherwise indicated, are taken from the Holy Bible, New International Version®, NIV®. Copyright ©1973, 1978, 1984, 2010 by Biblica, Inc.™ Used by permission of Zondervan. All rights reserved worldwide. www.zondervan.com

Scripture quotations marked (KJV) are taken from the *King James Version* of the Bible. (Public domain)
Scripture quotations marked "MSG" or "The Message" are taken from The Message. Copyright 1993, 1994, 1995, 1996, 2000, 2001, 2002. Used by permission of NavPress Publishing Group. http://www.navpress.com/
Scripture quotations marked "NASB" are taken from the New American Standard Bible®, Copyright © 1960, 1962, 1963, 1968, 1971, 1972, 1973, 1975, 1977, 1995 by The Lockman Foundation.
Used by permission. www.Lockman.org

Cover & Interior Design: Christine Lewis
Author Photo: Garth Wunch

www.jeremymahood.com

To my Dad, Kitchener

Founding Pastor of All Nations Church
Sudbury, Ontario

The Rev. H.H.K Mahood 1916-1983

"He being dead, yet speaketh"
Hebrews 11:4 (KJV)

Contents

Introduction i

Aisle One: God's Blueprint 1

Aisle Two: Designing in 3D 19

Aisle Three: Sign the Contract; Seal the deal 44

Aisle Four: Take it to the Junk Yard 70

Aisle Five: Renovate and Redecorate 103

Aisle Six: The Smart House, Wired for Communication ... 129

Aisle Seven: Your Lifetime Guarantee 155

The Relationship Prayer 169

Acknowledgments 174

INTRODUCTION

After five years since *The Relationship Depot* was released, I have had many readers share how the books influenced their approach to marriage and relationships. I like to think they found the tools they had been searching for to build a solid foundation.

The second edition has not changed much, but we did add a Study Guide to help put into action the suggestions I have offered. The Study Guide can be used individually, as a couple or as a small group. Each chapter offers a set of questions that help to explore what you are using to build, fix or maintain your relationship.

The Relationship Depot book gives you the tools to build a strong, healthy, loving relationship so you can live in your dream marriage together for a lifetime.

Much like building a solid structure, we go to the hardware store to get the right materials and tools. When you neglect to create a strong foundation for your relationship, all the time energy and effort you put into the relationship is compromised by the lack of a strong foundation. "Being in love" is not foundation enough to build a relationships that lasts.

The Relationship Depot, provides the wisdom of God, the one who created us, and His foundational plans upon which to build a relationship that lasts a lifetime. Build your relationship God's way and you have God's lifetime guarantee that your relationship will withstand any storm.

I have officiated at well over 500 weddings. Most couples who get married are well intentioned when they say their vows, they mean what they say. However, the divorce rate continues to rise. The simple, but painful truth is that people have chosen to build their relationships on the shifting sands of popular opinion, societal norms, and have avoided following the blueprint for relationships that has been handed down through the ages in God's word, the Bible. Divorce is an epidemic of "spiritual' proportions in our culture and in our churches. *The Relationship Depot* can help you sort out all the confusing and conflicting messages society gives about marriage and divorce. This book can also help you experience Gods healing for a broken heart; a heart torn and fractured by divorce and multiple sexual relationships. There is a reason God says that he hates divorce. The sooner you shut the door on the divorce option, the healthier you will be.

As you read this book, you will come to understand Gods heart on the subject of relationships. God made you to be in a relationship with himself and others, and specifically that special someone with whom you can build a life and a family. God's desire for you is to be safe, fulfilled, loved and respected in your relationship. God has designed a covenant just for relationships, a covenant sealed with blood. This covenant comes into place with the sexual union of a man and a woman and it is God's iron clad guarantee of his presence in your married life.

Use the biblical building code to construct your life together. Accept God's warranty for your marriage, and you will have built a relationship that lasts a lifetime.

Aisle One
God's Blueprint

God, in his divine plan, created you to be with a partner – not alone, but with one person and for that relationship to be a permanent bond. Yet society tells you differently. You are told that it is okay to have sex before marriage, to choose a mate based on sexual attractiveness, and to jump from bed to bed looking for the right one, test driving the relationship before you buy.

I never intended to get married. As a young man I planned to spend my life singing in night clubs and taking home women who were crazy enough to spend a night or two with me, and then moving on to the next bar and the next girl. Every night was going to be a party. God had not yet convinced me that his plan was better than mine.

It was my wife, Eileen, who introduced me to God's blueprint for marriage, but not at first. We met in a Nanuet, New York nightclub, right next to the Tapanzee Bridge; about 20 miles north of New York City. I was the entertainer playing my multiple key boards and singing the latest pop hits. She was a graduate operating room nurse working as a consultant in the medical industry. Eileen stood out in the crowd and before long I was picking on her, telling jokes at her expense and downright embarrassing her in a large room full of party goers. On my break I went right over to the table full of girls where she was sitting and specifically thanked Eileen for being a good sport. I still recall the excitement when our knees touched under the small round table.

I confidently asked her out on a date and we kept on dating, but I remained aloof. Eileen was persistent. Things got serious. I began to distance myself. Eileen was persistent. I was difficult. You guessed it, Eileen was persistent. Making a marriage commitment for me was difficult. I was reluctant to cut off my options, or more honestly, I was not able to express real intimacy. That was the late 70s and we remain happily married today, thanks to Eileen's persistence.

No woman has ever loved me like Eileen. What struck me was the fact that she loved me for who I was, not for what I did. She loved me; not the musician, the funny guy, the guy with the talent or the guy with the money. She simply loved whatever it was she saw in me. I discovered every man's dream, to be with a woman who would still love him even when his failures and insecurities rose to the surface of his life. This realization did not come until many years later, but it was this quality of love that Eileen shared that became the catalyst for me to allow God to begin to do his work in me. I could be weak, vulnerable and insecure before Eileen and before God, and still be safe and loved.

When Eileen and I married we had no instruction manual. I never read the instructions for building or renovating anything so why would I need to read instructions for marriage? Truthfully, I did not have a clue what I wanted. I have also discovered that most other people have no idea either.

I had no idea how to build and maintain a marriage.

It was many years later before I discovered that there is an instruction manual for marriage, written by the inventor of marriage. Everything you need to know about the foundation principles for a healthy marriage God wrote down for us in the Bible. Marriage is God's idea. He created the possibility of it for a very specific purpose. When we fulfill that purpose we have a healthy, secure and happy marriage. When we fail to fulfill the Creator's intended purpose for marriage, we have what we see in most of the western world; marriages full of distress and immense pain, well-meaning people entering into a marriage relationship that is destined to fail because they have never discovered the true purpose of being married. Marriage is often assumed as something we just instinctively know how to do, but it is not. Take a look around you and you will see how good our marital instincts are. Divorce is big business.

Marriage is so sacred because it reflects the divine.

The reason why marriage is vitally important to believers in Jesus Christ is that it is designed to be a reflection of who God is. Marriage is so sacred because it reflects the divine.

The scripture says when you are united together as man and woman, you become one flesh. The statement "one flesh" is vital to our understanding of the marriage union and its purpose. There is a reason why God said we are not to separate that one flesh. There is no way to separate without great pain or heartache, emotional or spiritual bleeding. If we could see inside the spirit of people who have been divorced, or who have had multiple sexual or emotional relationships, we would be horrified to see the tangled emotional mess that resides there.

When we go back to the first book of the Bible, we learn just how it all started. God had spent several days creating the heavens and the earth, and then he made a man. And the Lord God said, **"it is not good for the man to be alone."** (Genesis 2:18) We can imagine Adam heaving a sigh of relief when God brought Eve into the picture.

God created the first earthly relationship

In Genesis we learn how man and woman came to co-exist together.

> **Now the LORD God had formed out of the ground all the beasts of the field and all the birds of the air. He brought them to the man to see what he would name them; and whatever the man called each living creature, that was its name. So the man gave names to all the livestock, the birds of the air and all the beasts of the field.**
> Genesis 2:19-20

What a day's job! But for Adam, no suitable helper was found. Animals just did not fill the void. So God said, "I will make a helper." It is important to clarify here that 'helper' in the original language, means someone who comes alongside, not a servant, cook or someone to do the laundry. God said, "I will make somebody to come alongside the man, a partner, so he is not alone."

> So the LORD God caused the man to fall into a deep sleep; and while he was sleeping, he took one of the man's ribs and closed up the place with flesh. Then the LORD God made a woman from the rib he had taken out of the man, and he brought her to the man.
> Genesis 2:21-22

"YES!" said Adam, "I could spend some time with that thing you just made out of my rib," as he beholds the most perfect naked female that has ever existed in the world. Adam then says,

> **This is now bone of my bones and flesh of my flesh; she shall be called woman, for she was taken out of man.**
> Genesis 2:23

God made them Adam and Eve. However, in a secular pluralistic society some do accept that guys want to be together, and girls want to be together. That is the prerogative of a secular, pluralistic society, but for Christians, God says a marriage is the union between a male and female. The next verse goes on to explain how the man and woman will unite.

> **That is why a man leaves his father and mother and is united to his wife and they become one flesh.**
> Genesis 2:24

This is a really critical moment in understanding relationships and marriage. Each of us leaves our original family and creates a new family. We belong to our new family and essentially must trust and be committed to that new family. For a healthy marriage bond, a couple must commit to leave behind their family of origin to the extent that they become free to be a couple, devoid of outside influence from the original parents. Far too many spouses still have one foot remaining in their parent's door, while they have one foot in the door of their new home. There must be an emotional leaving that frees the human spirit up to form a new kind of matrimonial bond. I love this next verse:

> **The man and his wife were both naked, and they felt no shame.**
> Genesis 2:25

There was no shame back then, no sin to feel bad about, none of the problems we have today. They were comfortable being their vulnerable selves; completely exposed and completely safe, nothing hidden, no fear and none of that debilitating emotion of shame.

> **Then God said, Let us make mankind in our image, in our likeness, and let them rule over the fish of the sea and the birds of the air, over the livestock, over all the earth, and over all the creatures that move along the ground. So God created mankind in his own image, in the image of God he created them; male and female he created them.**
> Genesis 1:26-27

God created the male and female in his image and the first relationship in his image.

Relationships are God's work of art; we do not get to mess with his art.

Here is another translation of this story as Jesus tells it, and when Jesus speaks, we need to pay attention.

Aisle One | God's Blueprint

> "Haven't you read," he replied, "that at the beginning the Creator 'made them male and female, and said, 'For this reason a man will leave his father and mother and be united to his wife, and the two will become one flesh'? So they are no longer two, but one flesh. Therefore what God has joined together, let no one separate.
> Matthew 19:4-6

This is a really big clue to the purpose and intent of the marriage relationship. Jesus is saying that humankind was made in his image and likeness. Man and woman take on a God-like quality of unity. When they come together in marriage they are an earthly reflection of the divine relationship of the Godhead, the unique quality of being Father, Son and Holy Spirit. Marriage is designed to reflect that indivisible union on earth. The three in heaven are one. The two on earth become one. Male and female together, always working in harmony for good, are a reflection of who God is.

Now that is one high and mighty purpose for an earthly marriage relationship. If you think the primary purpose of marriage is legal sex, you are mistaken. If you think the primary purpose of marriage is to make you happy, wrong again. If you think the primary purpose of marriage is making babies, wrong. The primary purpose in God creating the marriage relationship is so that it can be a mirror image on earth of what God is in heaven. The master Creator, with all that creative power, is shaping us to be like Jesus, bringing love into the world. The same principle of union is found with Jesus as both man and God. He was both human and divine.

> **I and the Father are one.**
> John 10:30

Jesus says while I am divine, while I am still God…yet here I am on earth, I hurt, I bleed, I cry.

Your relationship is to be a reflection of that kind of unity. It can sometimes seem impossible to create unity with two different people. When my wife and I came together others might have thought this type of unity was impossible. I am the only child of immigrant parents, raised in stoic Irish ways, who married an American Catholic girl, with four siblings. But we did come together, with all our family of origin issues, with all our history, all our stuff, with all our experiences. I came into the relationship as an addict, to my wife who was not an addict. We came to this relationship with all our uniqueness, and over time and with God's help and intervention, we trust we are becoming a mirror of the unity of God.

You get to partner with God in creation.

Another thing that is so interesting about marriage is you get to partner with God in creation. That concept has always blown my mind. I heard Tony Campolo talk about this partnership in creation. He tells the story of how one little sperm out of a million gets to make a difference. There it is waiting at the starting gate with thousands of other little sperm. This is to be their big day. Suddenly they are propelled down a long dark canal; swimming for all they are worth, racing against the clock with the other little sperm, and the lucky one spots an egg. It swims and swims, yelling, "I did it!"

Aisle One | God's Blueprint

Out of a million sperm, in a nanosecond of time, one little sperm reaches an egg and life is created. If you ever doubt your significance...remember you are one in a million.

God says you get to create with him! You get to partner with him in creating life and for that reason alone, the marriage bond between male and female is a sacred bond. It is the only one that can create life. Now we interfere with that through scientific means like in-vitro fertilization. God's intention was that there would be a male and female, they would reflect the divine image, and they would have the opportunity to create together.

The Hebrew word for one is *echad*, which means "one; alike; altogether, or all at once." The very same word is used in Deuteronomy 6:4 for "the Lord is one." We are to come together as 'one' in our relationships. This does not mean that you lose your identity in relationship. God is very distinctive in what he does and who he is. His son, Jesus Christ, is very distinct. The work of the Holy Spirit transforms and changes us, and is very unique in what he does. You can state the uniqueness of the Godhead this way: he is the Father as to his divinity, he is the Son as to his humanity, he is the Holy Spirit as to his activity. Somehow, in a very mysterious way, divinity, humanity and activity come together as one. God, while three, is one God. Male and female, while two, may become one.

Relationships are primarily spiritual.

I came across a wise saying that has stuck with me for years. It goes like this: "we are not human beings on a spiritual journey but rather spiritual beings on a human journey." To grasp the significance of that statement is to revolutionize your life and relationships. Relationships are primarily spiritual. They are lived out in the physical and they encompass the emotional. It was God's idea to make woman out of the man. It was his idea to create their sexuality and put it all together so that relationships would be a spiritual reflection of Him.

It is all about God.

Marriage relationships exist to glorify God.

I hear it all the time, "I thought I was supposed to be happy!" Some think their primary purpose in life is to be happy and make others happy. Where did we get this way of thinking? The idea that God's primary purpose is to make us happy is not in the Bible.

The primary purpose of God working in your life is to make you holy. Many times the result of that holiness is happiness. But it never happens the other way around.

> **For he chose us in him before the creation of the world to be holy and blameless in his sight.**
> Ephesians 1:4

And again we read,

> **But just as he who called you is holy, so be holy in all you do;**
> 1 Peter 1:15

Holy in the scriptures means to be set apart for God's use. This is what God wants from you, that you would be available for his purposes. What God wants is for your marriage to be available to him. When we are available to God, it means we put him first, and live our lives under his priorities, not ours. To be holy before God means to search out his purpose for your marriage union. He definitely has a specific purpose for the two of you coming together. He will use both of you in each other's lives to heal, purify, restore, and polish you to such brilliance that your relationship becomes an accurate reflection of God on this earth.

Matthew writes about this "God First" principle and the resulting reward with simplicity and clarity.

> **But seek first his kingdom and his righteousness, and all these things will be given to you as well.**
> Matthew 6:33

When you put God first in all things, including your marriage relationship, God adds to your life the qualities of emotional richness, security and fulfilment that you so desire.

When you seek those qualities first before even God, you lose everything.

God's primary purpose is to make you holy.

The primary purpose of God working in your life is to make you a reflection of his divine image. To make you like Jesus Christ because Jesus Christ was the most perfect reflection of God's holiness known on earth. Jesus Christ was the perfect reflection of the divine in everything he said, and everything he did, he always obeyed the Father. He was always obedient. That is why he was called sinless.

This is God's writing, his story...we don't get to re-write it. Check this verse out in Romans:

> God knew what he was doing from the very beginning. He decided from the outset to shape the lives of those who love him along the same lines as the life of his Son. The Son stands first in the line of humanity he restored. We see the original and intended shape of our lives there in him. After God made that decision of what his children should be like, he followed it up by calling people by name. After he called them by name, he set them on a solid basis with himself. And then, after getting them established, he stayed with them to the end, gloriously completing what he had begun.
> Romans 8:28-29 (MSG)

First off, he says that God knew what he was doing from the very beginning. Now that should give some of us who are control freaks a reason to relax. God is at work here. God has a plan and had it from the beginning. He is not making it up as he goes along. Notice the second sentence. God is assuring us that it is his intention to shape our lives similarly to that of his son. This is God's promise to us and his most likely *shaping* instrument is going to be your spouse.

Check out the very last sentence: God has promised to stay with us to the end. Over difficult mountains or in devastating valleys, though you stumble, fall, quit, rest, go in the ditch, mess it up, whatever, you have God's assurance that he will complete his work in you. He will not abandon this process of holiness part way through, in the good times or in the bad.

God does not abandon, God completes!

Aisle One | God's Blueprint

Would you like to know what you can expect from a spiritually mature relationship with God and with others?

> **But the fruit of the Spirit is love, joy, peace, patience, kindness, goodness, faithfulness, gentleness and self-control.**
> Galatians 5:22-23

When God is allowed to work through each of you, when his Spirit is able to build character in you, you receive the fruit of the Spirit.

Look at the attributes the Holy Spirit has pledged to produce in your life. Here they are, all lined up. Is this not what you desire in a relationship?

Love...unconditional, without strings, when you fail, when you succeed, held tightly in God's firm hand surrounded by his majesty and mighty power.

Joy...like a bubbling spring welling up from deep inside your person, a lightness of spirit, an absence of heaviness and new way to view pain.

Peace...the constant assurance that God never changes even though circumstances may be uncertain. When I cannot trace God's hand, I can always trust his heart and rest in unchanging never ending love.

Patience...to be unhurried, to take time to stop and smell the roses, to mentor, to help others, to value another's time above my own, to give others space to grow, to let God work at his pace.

The Relationship Depot

Kindness...to smile, to overlook a fault, to accept the blame when it is truly yours, to never point your finger but always open your heart.

Goodness...seeking that which is morally sound and upright, to defend the right, to seek justice, to serve the poor in heart, the poor in spirit, and bind up the broken hearted.

Faithfulness...to be known as one who is reliable, respectful, who can be counted on, who never wavers and is always ready to help.

Gentleness...with a tender heart, an antidote to the chaos and noise of this world, a safe haven for the wounded even when the wounds are of their own making, a person to whom children would run.

Self-control...rising above the immediate emotion to make peace, planning ahead for the journey, staying calm under the pressures of life, constantly consistent, unflappable, ready.

This is God's promise to you in your relationships, if you will build it according to his blueprint. You will come together with one person, stay, grow and mature together as a couple. Together, both as individuals and as a couple, you will reflect the holiness and the beauty that is God. If we are to be like God in marriage then we start with two people, joined in a way to become one. They still have their individual selves but in coming together in marriage they join to become one, like God's multiple Spirit.

In the Garden of Eden, there were three present, Adam, Eve and God. There was also joy. So, if God is central in a marriage today, there also will be joy. Without God, a true and full oneness is not possible. Together they make themselves available to God for his purposes, and over time become an accurate reflection of the divine Spirit so that the world will see Jesus in them.

The world is craving for relationships that satisfy. God is craving for couples who will let him work in their lives so that the world may know who he is. Will you make a commitment right now to let God direct and grow your marriage, or your future marriage? Would you accept the challenge to build a relationship, not on your terms, or about what you think you want, but a relationship based on what God wants and according to his blueprint?

The Relationship Depot

Review

In the first chapter the concept that marriage is sacred to God has been introduced. Marriage is spiritual. Taking this important step in our lives requires us to be mature enough to honour the covenant of marriage, a covenant without an escape clause.

The marriage covenant is sacred because the unity formed by the husband and wife reflects God. As a man and woman come together with their lives they are made one spiritually.

The relationship we create as husband and wife allows us the privilege to grow toward God; to grow back to the relationship God intended for Adam and Eve in the Garden of Eden. Uniting with the person God has chosen for us by leaving our mother and father is an important step in our maturity. Families are important to God, reflecting the original family.

God's blueprint for building this significant, lifelong covenant is solid. Deviating from the blueprint only creates structural problems for many generations in that family. Those stages to building a solid relationship are laid out for us in his Word.

Bible Instructions

> **That is why a man leaves his father and mother and is united to his wife and they become one flesh.**
>
> Genesis 2:24

Aisle One | God's Blueprint

Haven't you read," he replied, "that at the beginning the Creator made them male and female, and said, 'For this reason a man will leave his father and mother and be united to his wife, and the two will become one flesh'? So they are no longer two, but one flesh. Therefore what God has joined together, let no one separate.

Matthew 19:4-6

Building activities:

1. What are the intentions for your marriage?

2. What is God's intention for your marriage?

3. How do your intentions and God's intentions compare?

4. Has the primary purpose in your marriage been something other than Godly love, possibly security? Sex? Family expectations? If you have not made it Godly love, how could you bring that into your relationship?

5. List steps you could take to restore God's primary purpose for your marriage.

6. The last sentence commands that "what God has joined together let no one separate". Do you harbor any ideas about what could justify separating what God has joined together? Be honest.

Aisle Two
Designing in 3D

It was no surprise when the grade 11 Family Studies class in front of me was eager to hear what I had to say about sex. High School students always seem eager to talk about sex. My opening question was an attention grabber: "Girls, have you ever wondered why you can go out with a boy, spend time with him, have sex with him, and when you break up he has a new girl the next day?" They're often mystified how some boys can just 'move on' without any apparent emotional distress. This scenario carries on into adulthood. Men and women get intimacy and sex all mixed up.

Author, Jim Talley, in his book *Too Close Too Soon* explains that it takes much longer for a man to progress to the genuine commitment stage in a relationship than it does a woman. An emotional healthy woman needs to be in love to share her sexuality with a man. A man does not. A man who is only seeking sexual gratification has learned that he can get sex if he tells a woman that he loves her. The woman believes he is sharing feelings like hers and surrenders her body. The man enjoys having sex, never thinking he is making a commitment. For the man, a break up is not so devastating because he has no

The Relationship Depot

deep emotions invested in the relationship in the first place. On the other hand, the woman is brokenheartd and feeling used only for sexual gratification. The reason why there are so many broken relationships and wounded people in our society can be traced to the fact that they are having sex too soon. Women do not wait long enough before engaging in sexual activity to be certain that men are making a genuine emotional commitment to the relationship. Men want to have sex first and worry much later about having a lasting relationship in their lives. For a healthy relationship to grow into maturity, sexual activity in a relationship needs to be the final, not first, connection point.

There are many pressures that complicate the development of healthy relationships. While we are out looking for a connection, we encounter an over-sexed culture. Sex is everywhere. In most advertising, whether print, television, movies or video games, sex is used to attract our attention.

I remember when I was in university and I opened my first copy of Penthouse magazine that actually showed a naked woman, with nothing hidden. I was in a band and this guy would come up from New York City with his car loaded with men's magazines, pictures of real action. We would sneak out on our break and give him 50 bucks for a magazine.

Today, the television broadcasts abusive sex all day long. Young children and pre-teens are being exposed to the most abnormal sex-crazed culture we have ever lived in. Yet we ask ourselves, why do I have trouble connecting? Why do I have trouble with intimacy? Why is my mind so distorted about all of this?

Aisle Two | Designing in 3D

We have created a society in the last thirty years where we are oversexed and oversaturated. Clothing manufacturers are creating outfits for pre-teens that years ago would not have even been seen on a college student. Parents are not gate-keeping these messages, but are permitting their kids to wear this stuff. Music television is saturated with sexual innuendo that young males and females are watching from early childhood. Tell me, what does an overly sexually stimulated eight or nine year old do with those feelings?

In his book, *All Grown Up, With No Place To Go*, and his follow up book, *The Hurried Child*, David Elkind proposes that parents and society have been forcing kids into a form of maturity that is beyond their emotional capacity to handle. I read these books at least twenty years ago, yet you would think, by the state of our society, that Elkind wrote them just last week.

The main-streaming of pornography, which is essentially voyeuristic, self-stimulating and abusive, is everywhere. Examples of friendship, commitment and physical passion are almost impossible to find. In fact, the internet and our cable companies would not survive if it was not for the mainstreaming of pornography. The economic survival of cable, satellite and internet is largely dependent on the downloading and purchasing of pornography. Who is viewing all of this? Why is it such an epidemic? Could it be that we have strayed so far from God's ideals that we are on a collision course with hell?

Today we are facing an unprecedented epidemic of adults who are unable to form emotional attachments.

We must get back to God's design for intimacy. That means starting with your relationship to him, and continues with developing loving, healthy emotional and physical relationships with each other.
To continue with sexual relationships outside the safety of an unbreakable covenant of marriage is to continue to starve ourselves emotionally. More sex is not the solution to our emotional starvation. The solution is greater intimacy, and that can only begin with God.

In the same way that a newborn child needs food and nurturing to survive, we also need emotional connection to fully develop. There is a term in child protection services called 'attachment disorder'. This term is applied when children are deprived of maternal bonding and it significantly impacts their ability to develop their full emotional and physical potential. Today, we are facing an unprecedented epidemic of individuals who are failing to bond due to intimacy starvation. Our need for emotional connection reflects God's design for us to have relationships with each other. Coming together in spiritual, emotional and physical relationship is to be a mirror of divine intimacy. The crisis we face in this generation is the sex- crazed society that has separated the physical sex act out from the emotional and spiritual parts. This 'deconstruction' of sex into merely a physical act, devoid of vulnerability and commitment, is at the root of the desecration of marriages in our world today.

Having sex too soon in a relationship only <u>adds</u> to our wounds.

Sexual activity in a relationship needs to be the final connection point for a healthy relationship to grow into maturity, not the first. Congregation members Richie and Janet were struggling with real intimacy when they came for counsel. After being married for six years, they were hardly spending time together.

"When we first met, we couldn't stand to be apart," Janet explained. "We were happy doing anything so long as we were together and the sex was great."

Now the two were feeling disconnected and struggling to find similar interests at this point in their marriage. I can guarantee you that Richie and Janet had sexual relations very early in their dating relationship. Their story follows a well-defined pattern in our current culture. Meanwhile some Christian couples, like Jack and Cheryl, who fought against current culture and dated for six years without developing a sexual relationship before marriage, continue to enjoy a loving and affectionate relationship after 38 years.

Something has gone terribly wrong, because so few couples ever experience the love and respect they so deeply crave.

Dr. Emerson Eggerichs and his wife Sarah share in their book, *Love and Respect*, that men may be even more interested in being respected then being loved. Every boy who has not been abused or abandoned has the same dream: somewhere there is a woman with whom they can share all of the secrets of their life, and who will respect them for it. They hope to be with somebody that they can be real with, even when she sees their weaknesses and failures, and how messed up they can be. She is still going to love them.

Talking just to the men here, imagine waking up every morning and being loved by a woman who will continue to love you even when you take off your emotional mask. Even in your weaknesses, failures, and messes she will continue to respect you.

Every girl who has not been abandoned or abused has the same dream: *somewhere there is a man that I can give all of myself to who will keep me safe and cherish me*.

Now just talking to the ladies, imagine feeling totally safe in a relationship; regardless of how you are on any given day, you will be loved. No matter how threatening a situation you may face, your husband will be there beside you. He will protect you and keep you safe. He will always cherish you and treat you more special than anything else in his life, including his car or his golf clubs! That is some kind of love.

God created those cravings for love and respect in us and has a sure-fire way to meet those cravings when we listen and follow what he has to offer us. But casual sexual relationships complicate those needs in us, and in turn, will result in emotional damage or emotional junk.

Add to this situation, young men and women growing up in fractured households where there is great instability. Young women who grow up without a strong male influence, due to a father's death, desertion, or emotional unavailability, often take one of two paths in relationships. Either they become sexually active at a very young age because they are looking for the intimacy they should have received from a positive male figure, an intimacy not tied to sexuality. Or they go the other way and become sexually cold and distant.

Aisle Two | Designing in 3D

Young men who grow up in a home without a positive male influence but had a dominant female influence may also take two different paths in their relationships. They may take on the characteristics of what we would label being macho, a ladies' man or a player. These men abuse women as a way to define their manhood. Or they may take another path and reject relationships with women altogether, feeling safer in a relationship with other men.

As Christians we should know that we were designed by God primarily to have an intimate relationship with him. That means we were designed to be connected with God at the deepest core of our being. The emotional effect of being connected with God, at the very core of our being, is that we will feel safe. There is a security in knowing that God knows all about us and still loves us. If God loves me for who I am, then I can be less demanding of my other relationships.

Intimacy has been defined by the saying *into-me you-see*! God sees into-you, loves you and invites you to go and love others, and not be afraid to let them see-into-you-too! It is the love of God in us that we offer others. His love is the launching pad for our love. We love others from an established position of spiritual security.

In the early days of singing concerts in church, one of my favourite songs was Bill and Gloria Gaither's *I Am Loved* and it describes that kind of love.

> I am loved, I am loved; I can risk loving you; For the One who knows me best; Loves me most; I am loved, you are loved; Won't you please take my hand; We are free to love each other; We are loved.

This ability to connect on a deeply intimate level with God and each other began with God making the first move. God removed any barriers to that intimate connection with himself through Jesus Christ's sacrificial death on the cross. His death, paying the penalty for our sin, broke down the barrier that existed between God and humankind. We need to acknowledge that we have gone our own way without regard for God and his laws. There can be no greater intimacy with God than the Holy Spirit living inside us. When you and I surrender our lives to Christ, there must be willingness on our part to be vulnerable, take the risk, in faith, that God will do what he says he will do in our lives. When we acknowledge our past failures, sins, and shortcomings we are opening ourselves to God and trusting he will take care of us spiritually and emotionally.

Intimacy can only be cultivated in an atmosphere of vulnerability.

Without vulnerability, any relationship we may have will not be a reflection of true intimacy. Vulnerability is when we expose all of ourselves. Jesus Christ hung on the cross, open, naked and vulnerable before the world to demonstrate his love for us. Now he asks us to respond to his vulnerability by being vulnerable ourselves.

There is a distinct relationship between intimacy and vulnerability. One of the reasons why we fail to achieve true intimacy is due to a failure to be vulnerable with each other. Most of us desire true intimacy, but we are afraid to face our shame and experience true vulnerability. Most of us have never been in an environment where we have felt emotionally safe, so we never reveal all the experiences and characteristics of ourselves. When we are vulnerable, we lose control. But if we won't give up control, we will never experience true intimacy. Being comfortable with your vulnerability is the ultimate intimacy. Reaching a stage in your life's journey where you can say to yourself, and anyone else who will listen, "it's ok to be just the way I am", and mean it without sarcasm or rancour, is real maturity.

God's vulnerability to us as humans is seen in Christ's crucifixion.

> **But God demonstrates his own love for us in this: While we were still sinners, Christ died for us.**
> Romans 5:8

So, God goes first. He exposes his desire to love us by breaking down any barriers that might prevent us from experiencing his love. He did this by taking the sins, which alienate us from God, and vicariously carrying them with him to the cross. They were eliminated when he was crucified; and he did all of this without asking us, during a time of spiritual alienation and isolation from God. As the apostle Paul tells us, Christ went first, he made the first move, before any of us had an opportunity to clean ourselves up, have a shave or put on make-up. God took the risk and loved us just the way we are.

This act by God s a demonstration of true vulnerability. While you were consumed with your own self-importance, climbing the social ladder, building your own kingdom, following your own dreams, doing life *My Way*, God, in Christ Jesus, took a risk for you, that one day you would desperately recognize your need for his love and forgiveness. When you come to him in your darkest hour looking for help, he would say to you:

"Done! Finished! I took care of it for you 2000 years ago. I've been waiting for you. What took you so long?"

There is another aspect that can bring death to a relationship and that is our attitude of self-sufficiency, namely believing that we can meet our needs on our own. The church at Laodicea said:

> **We are rich, increased with goods and have need of nothing.**
> Revelation 3:17

Some churches propagate two very dangerous teachings about needs and self-sufficiency. The first goes like this: "If you were just spiritually *mature*, you wouldn't have any needs," or "If you just had real faith then you wouldn't have any needs."

The second teaching states: "You don't need anyone but God to meet your needs. You should never need anyone but Him." The God who saw Adam's need of a *helper* is the same God who sees your need. God often uses human relationships to meet many of your needs.

If we follow these false teachings we're going to cut ourselves off from the *gifts of grace* God has for us. Everything he wanted us to receive from others we will miss because we deceived ourselves into believing we did not need anyone else. And if we think we do not need others, we will not realize that they need us.

"I don't need you, so why do you need me?" The truth is we do need each other, and if we persist in our pride and self-sufficiency, we will become resistant to God's flow of goodness in our lives and miss out on many of his blessings.

Paul writes about his own experience with God meeting his needs.

> I have received full payment and even more; I am amply supplied, now that I have received from Epaphroditus the gifts you sent. They are a fragrant offering, an acceptable sacrifice, pleasing to God. And my God will meet all your needs according to the riches of his glory in Christ Jesus.
> Philippians 4:18-19

While he explains in the last line that God will meet all your needs, from the never-ending depth of the riches that are Christ's, Paul also states in the opening paragraph that God has supplied his need through the gifts that were sent him by way of Epaphroditus. God saw that Paul's needs were met and it was God who commissioned another human to meet those needs.

I remember the day I overheard a woman telling my Dad that God was not enough for her, she needed a man. She promptly got herself involved in a relationship. It was damaging to her family and to her witness as a Christian. For years I was critical of her actions. I was taught to believe that all I needed was Jesus, nothing more. There is a truth to that statement, yet too many times it has been distorted. What is true is that Jesus is all you need for eternal salvation. You need nothing more than to believe in the finished work of Jesus on the cross for your eternal life.

> For it is by grace you have been saved, through faith - and this not from yourselves, it is the gift of God - not by works, so that no one can boast.
> Ephesians 2:8-9

The Relationship Depot

God meets our need for salvation entirely on his own. It is his gift to each of us who choose to accept it. There is no cost to us but repentance (acknowledging our wrong doing, turning around and going the other way) and receiving by faith, God's gift of salvation. You and I have physical and emotional needs that God designed to be met by other humans. The issue with the woman who believed she needed a man is that she pursued the relationship on her own, without God, and she found the wrong man. God has pledged to meet all our needs but we must let him do that on his own terms, in his own way, and perhaps most difficult to accept, in his own time.

God therefore ordained three divine relationships to fulfill our earthly needs: Marriage, Family and the Church. Since God's method of meeting our needs can come through marriage, the family and the church, it's no surprise that our adversary will make every effort to steal, kill, and destroy these three institutions. Just as surely as God says, "I will create," the Devil says, "I will destroy."

Marriage is under attack with families under great stress as we try to redefine how blended families function and explain to children why their friend has two daddies. Church attendance now seems to be only one of many options available on a weekend. Between the devil, our current culture, and our own earthly desires, mixed in with some apathy, we are shaking the pillars of stability in our world today.

A commercial about an internet service boasts 'you can have the perfect hook-ups with no commitments'. No contract, no term, surf with freedom. Sounds like our terms for dating. Just hook up and be a sex buddy for the night. No contract, no term, surf with freedom.

Aisle Two | Designing in 3D

The damage being done to the human spirit every day adds up to a tsunami of psychic pain. This out-of-control sexuality is fracturing marriages, damaging children and costing our economy billions of dollars.

My wife brought a deeper intimacy to our relationship. We met when I was a musician in New York City. She wasn't bedazzled by the musician, bright lights, cars, fame or money. There was nothing there. She saw something behind all of that stuff. I learned that I could be absolutely the weakest guy in the world with her. I didn't have to be macho; I didn't have to pretend to be what I was not. She could see the real me and she never used or abused my weaknesses. That is why I am still with her 36 years later. It does not matter how busted up I come home, or the mistakes I've made, she still loves me. To my way of thinking, her actions toward me have been God's way of fostering greater intimacy in my life.

> **When the foundations are being destroyed, what can the righteous do?**
> Psalm 11:3

The answer to that question is we must get back to being obedient to God and His Holy word. We can start with obedience in the very area of our lives and relationships that is so very seriously under attack, namely true intimacy. The bible helps us out with the complexity of intimacy and sexuality. Let me take you back into the Old Testament to the Song of Solomon, one of the hottest books, that teaches us about love, intimacy and sexuality. Pastor Rob Bell's video entitled "Flame" teaches that there are three different Hebrew words for our English word "love" in the Song of Solomon.

> Thou art all fair, my love [RAYA]; there is no spot in thee.
> Song of Solomon 4:7 (KJV)

In the NIV it reads:

> **All beautiful you are, my darling [RAYA]; there is no flaw in you.**

RAYA translated literally means *friend* or *companion*. Someone you enjoy hanging out with, *soul mate* or someone you share a deep friendship with.

The word in verse seven for darling is RAYA. I know this RAYA feeling. After being married for 36 years my best friend and RAYA, my best companion, and my soul mate, is my wife. You can imagine that after so many years together there have been some really tough times in our relationship. Even in the really tough times of our marriage, my wife is still my RAYA. She is still my very, very best friend, and I would rather be with her than anybody else.

The second word used for love in the Song of Solomon is AHAVA, which means a sense of deep affection and a love that gives selflessly. It is the feeling of wanting to give to someone based on their needs. Your mind and your heart are bent toward your lover with passion and intensity. This is more profound than the romantic feelings, that 'in-love' experience we hear about so much.

Here is how Solomon uses the word AHAVA:

> **Many waters cannot quench love [AHAVA]; rivers cannot wash it away. If one were to give all the wealth of his house for love [AHAVA], it would be utterly scorned.**
> Song of Solomon 8:7

AHAVA is a love that leads to commitment. It is making a decision to join your life to the life of another. Solomon is talking about that deep affection that you have that makes your heart swoon. You cannot wait to be together, to hear their voice, to see their smile.

There is a third kind of love in chapter 1:2, called DOD. This love word means to *carouse*, to *rock*, or to *fondle*. It's the physical, sexual, erotic element in a relationship.

> **Let him kiss me with the kisses of his mouth - for your love [DOD] is more delightful than wine.**
> Song of Solomon 1:2

This love ignites something inside and makes something *really* happen inside you. This is the physical, erotic love. When you reach AHAVA love, you want to give physical pleasure in a reciprocal relationship. The passion of AHAVA ignites and can only be quenched by the physical touch of DOD.

Solomon uses these three different words for love. They describe friendship, affection and the physical part of love. What Rob Bell is able to illustrate so well in his video, is the need for us to experience all three love elements if we are to know the love God is talking about. The three love elements (flames) all come together as one. Have you ever tried to separate the flames of a fire; the blue from the green, from the orange? It's impossible.

It is interesting how God is a unity in diversity – Father, Son and Holy Spirit – and is still one God. Similarly the three loves are summed up as one love. One flame, burning all by itself, will never be as hot as all the flames burning together. A relationship that only expresses itself physically, through sex, without deep friendship and commitment, is going to burn out. Likewise, a relationship that has a commitment, but has lost the friendship and sexual passion, is also missing something.

We live in a world where there is a crisis of intimacy.

We were created by God to have friendship, commitment and physical passion bound up together in love. There is no such thing as true intimacy, without friendship, commitment and physical passion. There is a crisis of intimacy in our world. We do not seem to understand what it means anymore to experience true intimacy. We are not exactly sure what it is we are looking for, but we go looking anyways. We find ourselves living in a world of broken and wounded people, all looking for this special intimacy and too many are not willing to look where God tells us to look.

We face an avoidance of commitment because of relationship pain. In this culture of only physical passion where we try to be committed but fail, we often feel burned. We equate commitment with loss and pain. More and more people are actually afraid to make a commitment to another person. Many settle for recreational sex, which wounds their spirit and their self-esteem even more, and reinforces their belief that commitment brings with it, loss and pain.

You need to decide to make a difference in your own life. If you are single and just got out of a relationship that broke up, take the opportunity to just be single for about a year. Find out what real relationships are all about. Allow God to begin to heal you and work in you. Allow God to nurture you and strengthen that connection with him. Take a time out. Take a break. Allow God to search you (Psalm 139) and lead you. Pay attention to your spirit and mind.

Deepen your relationship with God and make that relationship your priority. Break the cycle of dependency on needing another person to define who you are; let God do that. He will do that for you and you will never see yourself in the same way again. Once you have been truly loved by God you will have the standard by which to judge the quality of all other loves. Do the homework necessary to find some people who are on the same journey as you. Go to a church, join a small group and be disciplined to not get involved in intimate conversations with the opposite sex. Those kinds of conversations lead toward behaviours you want to stay away from at this time. Get up close and intimate with God.

For men, it is sometimes hard to be intimate with God. Intimacy has primarily been based around being physical. God comes along and he wants to touch a man's spirit and many of us men do not know how to let that happen. As you find a few other guys who you feel safe with, your ability to be more vulnerable will surface. As you become more vulnerable, you will experience more intimacy, and your relationship with God will come alive.

The only person who can repair the human spirit is God.

In a relationship when you move right into DOD love, the physical kind of love, you are not protected emotionally. The damage that this does to the human spirit is only repairable by God who made us. You cannot repair a damaged spirit in therapy, and it will not be repaired anywhere else. Only God can heal the human spirit.

We were designed to be physically sexual human beings in a safe place. A man needs to commit to a woman that the sexual

The Relationship Depot

relationship will always be a safe place. The marriage bed will always be a safe place. It will never be violated or used in any way against the other person.

One of the things that my wife and I agreed on early in our marriage, was that we would never trade sex for anything. Sex was never to be a negotiating tool or a way to get material things. We agreed that sex would always be a special act that allows us the safety to be ourselves in the relationship, warts and all!

I do not believe that the church has done a good enough job of clarifying how important it is to establish all three aspects of love in our relationships. We always want to go to the physical. Here is what happens. DOD has so much power that it absolutely swamps the other two loves. When you base a relationship on DOD, with AHAVA and RAYA later, you compromise the foundation of the relationship. Every time you are together, having sex is the primary goal. A date goes something like this: watch part of the movie, have popcorn and talk for five minutes, then hit the sheets. When physical love becomes more important than the other two loves, deep affection and selfless giving never develop. Sex trumps everything.

So what happens in a relationship when the sex begins to lose its lustre? If you have a mature and balanced relationship, one where AHAVA and RAYA have been allowed to mature, your relationship will most likely survive just fine. If not, you may be just like Richie and Janet sitting in my office wondering what happened to the spark in your relationship. Or it completely breaks, and you are paying out big bucks to the divorce lawyers.

In the relationship where DOD love is no longer available, where friendship and trust were never developed, there is no AHAVA love to sustain a relationship. You may hear this described as 'falling out of love'.

When we violate God's principle to create a place of safety, a place of vulnerability in our relationships, we sabotage true intimacy. That is why God says you cannot break the covenant of marriage. God wants you to stay with it and work out your problems with each other. You are to invite God into that relationship. In that atmosphere of absolute safety, true intimacy will come.

Rabbi Menachem Schneerson states in his book *Toward a Meaningful Life*, that monogamy and longevity are the conditions for safety, where people are more likely to be open to intimacy. He reaffirms God's message that marriage to that one special person creates the safety for ongoing intimacy.

Darlene Zschech wrote these words for the song *Power of Your Love*. They could be used for your heart's prayer to God. They are some of the most intimate words offered to God that I have ever read.

> Lord I come to You; Let my heart be changed, renewed
> Flowing from the grace; That I've found in You
>
> Lord I've come to know; The weaknesses I see in me
> Will be stripped away; By the power of Your love
> Lord unveil my eyes; Let me see You face to face;
> The knowledge of Your love; As You live in me;
> Lord renew my mind;
> As Your will unfolds in my life In living every day;
> By the power of Your love

The Relationship Depot

> Hold me close; Let Your love surround me; Bring me near;
> Draw me to your side; And as I wait I'll rise up like the eagle;
> And I will soar with You;
> Your Spirit leads me on; In the power of Your love

This little line is from God to you – *Intimacy is an attitude of the heart*. It is not being touched or touching, it is not any of that. It is, however, wanting God and desiring closeness with God. Open your heart to God, right now. Choose an attitude of intimacy. Your life will soar like an eagle, believe me!

Review

The confusion between love and sex is rampant in our culture making it very hard to not be confused about real intimacy on which marriage is based. The bible clarifies the differences between sex and intimacy and how they play a role in romance and marriage.

David in the Song of Solomon poetically illustrates the different stages of love and intimacy. The Raya love of friendship, Ahava love of acceptance and DOD love of physical intimacy. Growing through those stages leads to the love God wants us to experience in the oneness of marriage. Messing with those loves and God's plan for developing real intimacy makes for challenging relationships.

Emotional connection is natural and healthy. It forms our bonding experience with others; firstly, with our parents, siblings and other family members, and developing real intimacy. Divine intimacy is an emotional bond.

Intimacy can only be cultivated in an atmosphere of vulnerability and the marriage relationship is the opportunity to experience that vulnerability. For some people, achieving true intimacy takes a lifetime. We try to escape through addictions, affairs and divorce but if we grow through our sin we will get to Christ's love in all its glory.

Biblical Instructions

> **But God demonstrates his own love for us in this: While we were still sinners, Christ died for us.**
>
> Romans 5:8

The Relationship Depot

I have received full payment and have more than enough. I am amply supplied, now that I have received from Epaphroditus the gifts you sent. They are a fragrant offering, an acceptable sacrifice, pleasing to God. And my God will meet all your needs according to the riches of his glory in Christ Jesus.

Philippians 4:18-19

**You are altogether beautiful, my darling;
there is no flaw in you.**

Song of Solomon 4:7

**Many waters cannot quench love;
rivers cannot sweep it away.
If one were to give all the wealth
of one's house for love,
it would be utterly scorned.**

Song of Solomon 8:7

**Let him kiss me with the kisses of his mouth—
for your love is more delightful than wine.**

Song of Solomon 1:2

Aisle Two | Designing in 3D

Building activities:

1. How was intimacy shown in your family while growing up? Was there honest sharing? Shouting? Affection?

2. How does it compare to how God instructs us to be close to others?

3. Part of intimacy is vulnerability; do you accept who you are? Do you feel comfortable sharing who you are with others?

The Relationship Depot

4. How can God's acceptance of us when you were imperfect help you accept your spouse?

5. What type of love is most evident in your relationship? Raya – Ahava – DOD. Rate them.

6. What could you do to increase the intimacy you share with your spouse?

Aisle Three
Sign the Contract; Seal the Deal

Our marriage ceremony was performed on January 1st, at half-time of a college football game on television. We held it on the balcony of our New York City apartment overlooking the Hudson River. The judge, our neighbour and friend, left his apartment at the two-minute warning to make it to our balcony. Nicky, my drummer, his girlfriend, and Eileen's long-time friends, Janet and Joey, also joined us. The vows were repeated, rings were exchanged and the deal was sealed. We watched the end of the football game and promptly caught a flight to Disney World in Florida. We spent three days honeymooning before the opening of my next show back in New York.

The marriage covenant, the bonding of man and woman is God's intention.

The marriage covenant is a big deal to God. Like the warranty on any product you buy, the terms are solid. The size of the celebration is inconsequential to the agreement being entered.

The word covenant can be explained as an irrevocable deal,

sealed in blood, and the agreed upon punishment for breaking the deal is death of the offender. The punishment of death indicates the importance of this covenant, although today the respect and understanding we have of this sacred covenant is lost in the temptations of the world.

My lack of understanding of the marriage covenant I entered with Eileen on that January afternoon came clear to me many years later. When we got married, Eileen and I had pretty much abandoned all our Christian education and family traditions, especially in the area of our sexual behaviour. We joined our lives together legally but we didn't fully understand marriage, and certainly not God's design for marriage. We defined marriage by our own set of values, far removed from God's values. We were making up our own rules and seriously messing with God's intended design.

Eileen was raised in a very strong Roman Catholic environment with regular attendance at Mass, confession the night before, and a Catholic school education, including nursing school. She also experienced Catholic values lived out with her family. My background was in a strong Baptist family with church attendance every Sunday morning and evening. There was also an extra hour of Sunday school for good measure. I joined a mid-week Christian- focused kid's club similar to Boy Scouts, but with some 'Jesus' thrown in. Like Eileen, I also attended a church-based youth group as a teen. My upbringing was filled with a strong moral code and a healthy work ethic. My father was a pastor, so I also developed a strong knowledge of the Bible and what it teaches about God, life, morality, ethics, creation, and God's plan for our ultimate salvation through Jesus Christ.

Aisle Three | Sign the Contract; Seal the Deal

Despite my Christian upbringing, and even though I was married, I had no intention of being sexually faithful and boldly told my new wife. We both travelled for our work and I needed to continue defining myself by my sexual encounters. I guess we both believed in the institution of marriage, our way though. We had dated for three years before deciding to get married and had become best friends. Life with Eileen was fun and adventuresome; she was spontaneous and very, very bright. However, it did take me two years of marriage to finally make a commitment to be faithful sexually and I have honoured that commitment throughout the remainder of our marriage. It took some time but God finally had my attention and my heart in the covenant.

Paul wrote some profound words to the Romans about the state of their society.

> **They exchanged the truth of God for a lie, and worshiped and served created things rather than the Creator - who is forever praised.**
> Romans 1:25

Paul says that we have exchanged the truth of God for a lie. We no longer think that God has any say in our actions, including the acceptance of God's design for marriage. He challenges the Romans that they have worshiped and served created things rather than the Creator. In other words, we idolize what we create and elevate our creations to the highest place of authority. We are redefining life and its boundaries as we see fit and in so doing we are ignoring God and his design for creation. Continuing we read:

> **Furthermore, since they did not think it worthwhile to retain the knowledge of God, he gave them over to a depraved mind, to do what ought not to be done.**
> Romans 1:28

As a society, we have been drifting further away from having a positive, collective consciousness about the state of our world. In his landmark book, *How Shall We Then Live?* from over 35 years ago, Francis Shaeffer postulates that as a society nears the end of its life span, a significant theme emerges: a withdrawal from the belief that we are "all in this life, in this world together".

Society promotes the desire to be left alone to live in *personal peace and affluence* away from God and our brothers and sisters in Christ, leading us to self-will rather than God's will.

Each of us must get back to an understanding of God's design for marriage and begin to do our part to restore God's intention for our lives. While we do not want to force our beliefs on other people, we can make a choice to live out our own lives in compliance with God's design. Just think what society would look like if, one by one, couple by couple, decisions were made to follow God's design for marriage and sexuality. The divorce rate would plummet, unwanted pregnancies would decline dramatically, broken hearts and wounded spirits would be restored to wholeness, children would experience the joy of knowing their fathers, and the economic hardships caused by family disintegration would cease. This type of spiritual and emotional restoration is available to you and to our society if we will learn and implement God's design for marriage and sexuality.

Aisle Three | Sign the Contract; Seal the Deal

Covenants are really important to God.

God demonstrates the importance of covenants in several circumstances and in those very early days with Adam and Eve (Genesis 3:21). He wanted to protect them and cover their shame so he killed an animal and spilled blood and made a covering for them out of skin.

Blood is vital to any covenant.

Blood is vital to any covenant. The root of the word for covenant, *berith*, literally means *a cut where blood flows*. Maybe you made an early blood covenant as a kid. I remember making a little cut and putting our fingers together, making a promise to be best friends forever. That sharing of blood, even to bond you as friends, symbolized the commitment.

The purpose of a covenant is to create an ultimate binding agreement to which two parties agree. They dedicate themselves to giving each other loyalty, fidelity, protection, promotion and prosperity, with no escape clause. The price of breaking the covenant is death. You cannot break a blood covenant.

When God wanted to make a convent with Israel, again blood was spilled.

> When Moses went and told the people all the LORD's words and laws, they responded with one voice, 'Everything the LORD has said we will do.' Moses then wrote down everything the LORD had said. He got up early the next morning and built an altar at the foot of the mountain and set up twelve stone pillars

> representing the twelve tribes of Israel. Then he sent young Israelite men, and they offered burnt offerings and sacrificed young bulls as fellowship offerings to the LORD. Moses took half of the blood and put it in bowls, and the other half he sprinkled on the altar. Then he took the Book of the Covenant and read it to the people. They responded, 'we will do everything the LORD has said; we will obey'. Moses then took the blood, sprinkled it on the people and said, "This is the blood of the covenant that the LORD has made with you in accordance with all these words."
> Exodus 24:3-8

Notice how it says that Moses took half the blood and put it in bowls and the other half he sprinkled on the altar. Moses then read from the book of the covenant, the deal that God was making with his people of Israel. The people responded, "We will do everything the LORD has said; we will obey." Then Moses took the blood that he had reserved in the bowls, and sprinkled it on the people. There was blood on the altar to represent God. The same blood from the same animals was on the people. The covenant agreement is sealed with the blood and the Lord's words.

Another form of covenant ritual in the ancient world involved the cutting of arms and the mingling of the blood of each individual. The individuals would treat the wound in such a way that a scar would remain, thus giving public evidence that a blood covenant was entered into. Since the covenant was binding, there was a period of planning, usually one year, that preceded the making of the covenant.

Blood covenant ritual also involved cutting or dividing animals in two.

Aisle Three | Sign the Contract; Seal the Deal

The carcasses would then be used to create a pathway of blood that the individuals would walk through in their bare feet twice (Genesis 15:10; Jeremiah 34:18-20). The first walk symbolized death - the individual had died, his former identity had ended, and all his possessions previously agreed upon now belonged to the other. The second walk symbolized a new birth and a new agreed upon identity.

Circumcision is also a blood covenant. As a sign of God's covenant with Abraham in Genesis 15, all males living under the influence of Abraham were to be circumcised as a token of that covenant (Genesis 17:10). The cutting away of the foreskin of the penis and the subsequent spilling of blood was a physical demonstration of being set apart for God and his purposes. It was an act of obedience.

God may have invited the people of Israel to place this covenant of circumcision on the very part of the body that symbolizes pleasure, to be a constant reminder to them to be focused on their special relationship with God and not get lost in life's pleasures and vices.

The ultimate covenant relationship is exemplified by the union between Christ and his Church.

The ultimate covenant relationship is exemplified by the union between Christ and his Church, made possible by the shedding of blood on the cross.

> For you know that it was not with perishable things such as silver or gold that you were redeemed from the empty way of life handed down to you from your ancestors, but with the precious blood of Christ, a lamb without blemish or defect.
> 1 Peter 1:18-19

The Relationship Depot

God, desiring to make an irrevocable covenant of redemption with you, sent his own son Jesus to be the blood sacrifice, to seal the deal! God makes a commitment to your salvation that is so powerful it can never be broken, and so intimate that it involves the death of his Son. In a spiritual sense, the blood of Christ is sprinkled over you, when in faith you accept the covenant that God is making, a covenant to forgive all of your sin and reserve a place for you in his kingdom. This covenant with God does not require shedding of blood on your behalf; it is God's work and requires nothing of you but faith.

This covenant of faith between God and his church is remembered each week in the church service known as The Lord's Supper, Communion or the Eucharist. Paul quotes the words of Jesus from the Last Supper.

> **In the same way, after supper he took the cup, saying, "This cup is the new covenant in my blood; do this, whenever you drink it, in remembrance of me."**
> I Corinthians 11:25

Each time we drink of the grape juice or wine at communion, Jesus wants us to remember the price he paid to seal the deal, a covenant securing our eternal future, written in blood. In the next verse we are reminded of what this spiritual feast means.

> **For whenever you eat this bread and drink this cup, you proclaim the Lord's death until he comes.**
> I Corinthians 11:26

This is God's story sealed by God's blood. He is coming again for us, for those who believe. He will not abandon us, he has made a promise and he has sealed it by his own blood. The covenant between Jesus and you is sealed in blood, and he will never break his covenant with you, he says I love you with an everlasting love. Jesus also invites us to keep the covenants we make with each other.

Your sexuality is the binding activity for the marriage covenant.

Your sexuality is the binding activity for your marriage warranty. The Token of Virginity found in Deuteronomy 22:17-18 says that if a man married a woman and he suspected she was not a virgin, she needed to bring the bed sheet that showed the drops of blood from their first sexual union. Think about this: God's intention is that a male virgin would come together with a female virgin and there would be blood spilled as that little strip of flesh called a hymen, is ruptured. The blood would surround that union, and it would be an everlasting blood covenant of that marriage. God placed that little bit of skin there so that when it was ruptured by a committed relationship it would become an irrevocable covenant before God.

In covenant ceremonies, the two individuals entering into covenant cut themselves and mingled their blood. When a woman loses her virginity she bleeds and this blood goes onto the man's penis.

The man is in her blood, with her flesh on either side of him; a covenant ceremony of marriage, sealed by blood. Each time that couple comes together again in sexual intercourse, they are re-enacting their covenant.

Blood was part of the establishment of the covenant between a man and a woman, and this is symbolic of the blood of Christ that establishes the new covenant with us. It should stand as a constant reminder to them of the terms of that covenant, just as partaking of communion stands as a reminder of our covenant with Jesus.

When God says that he hates divorce, he never intended for covenants to be broken. In the Old Testament, people who committed adultery were stoned because they violated the blood covenant and the price for that was death. Centuries later we live in a world that continuously ignores and violates that covenant.

Proverbs 2:17 calls the marriage contract <u>the covenant of God</u>.

While giving wise counsel to young men, Solomon makes a comment about an adulterous woman. He wrote that she has left the partner of her youth and ignored the covenant she made before God. Solomon is saying that there is a marriage contract made before God and the adulterer has ignored that contract. Solomon's words are very clear; a person leaving their marriage partner is ignoring the covenant made before God.

Sexual intercourse is part of a covenant relationship. God designed it to happen between one man and one woman in a mutually exclusive relationship. It is a representation of the covenants made down through history, sealed in blood for time and eternity. That is why you read in scripture where God gets so upset when we disrespect and abuse this gift. God is a covenant-keeping God and he expects the same from us.

God invented sex.

God invented sex. We understand his intention right there in the Bible. He says it was "very good". In Genesis 1:26, the Hebrew words *zachar* meaning male and *nekebah* meaning female are expressly sexual, and literally mean *piercer* and one *pierced*. God is not embarrassed by sexual intercourse; it was his good creation.

Since God does not have gender, the obvious question here is, how does creating humans as sexual beings, male and female, reflect the image of God? The intimacy expressed by our sexual union is a reflection of the intimacy God has with himself as Father, Son, and Holy Spirit. It starts with how good God is at intimacy, and God gives that intimacy to us in our sexuality.

It could be said that when you are most appropriate in your sexual relationship, you are then the most perfect reflection of who God is. It is because you are a sexual being that you can come to know and understand intimacy. The physical intimacy, only achieved through our sexuality, is a reflection of the intimacy that God has within himself as the Godhead of Father, Son and Holy Spirit.

Scripture teaches that there is a perfect, complete and intimate union between God as Father, Son and Holy Spirit. The apostle John records these words of Jesus:

> My prayer is not for them alone. I pray also for those who will believe in me through their message, that all of them may be one, Father, just as you are in me and I am in you. May they also be in us so that the world may believe that you have sent me.
> John 17:20-21

Notice Jesus' bold prayer; his desire for us as men and women of faith is that we all may be one, just as Jesus is one with his father; that there may be an intimacy that resembles the oneness of God in Christ Jesus. The result of this oneness is people come to believe in Jesus and the God who sent him.

Our sexuality gives us the longing and the capacity for intimate relationships.

For this reason, some have said that our sexuality is the most God-like part of who we are as humans. In Genesis 1:31, God has built all this earthly stuff, threw stars into space, made moons, rivers, trees, and every beast. After all this creation, God said, it *was good*. Then he made a man and then a woman and he declared it was *Very Good*. Read this verse out loud:

> God saw all that he had made, and it was very good. And there was evening, and there was morning - the sixth day.
> Genesis 1:31

We can actually have fun having sex.

God created you to be physically intimate with a spouse. God also added a bit of a zing to our sexuality that I do not think he gave to the animals. You can actually have fun having sex. He added the orgasm. Sex is not just purely functional either. Sex is more than getting the deed done and getting the sperm connected to the egg. God added something very unique to sex. He added that uniqueness to your physical sensations as you come together with your spouse, when you are touched in an erogenous zone that makes you feel

Aisle Three | Sign the Contract; Seal the Deal

sooooo good, and you can feel it heading out of control driving towards a climax. God added that! He added climaxes for our enjoyment and our pleasure. No wonder he declared that when he made man and woman it was *very good*.

Here is the problem.

When God tied an emotional and physiological response to our sexuality, he created the capacity for tremendous pleasure, but with that pleasure there is great danger. For God to give you that kind of physical pleasure with another, there is incredible danger for misuse.

Advertisers use this emotion to sell their products. Just suggest sex in a commercial and you can sell men almost anything! Advertisers know the emotion they want to trigger in men. It works all the time. There is no functional purpose to placing an attractive woman in short shorts and a halter top in a car commercial unless, of course, you want to tie a man's emotional stimulation to the brand name of your product. Likewise, if you want to get women's attention, connect it to romance. Spin some romance into it and make that product look like there is a knight in shining armour coming through to rescue that woman.

A deodorant company captured this concept with a television commercial. They placed a muscular football player, minus his shirt, on a horse inviting women, "look at me, now look at your man, and now look at me. Your man doesn't look like me". The implication is that a man could smell like the sexy man and that their deodorant will transform him into a knight in shining armour.

We are up against a massive system that is trying to distort our sexuality. Manipulating you becomes easy once that sexual self is removed from God's intention. Paul writes to the Corinthians about this problem.

> **Just because something is technically legal doesn't mean that it is spiritually appropriate.**
> I Corinthians 6:12 (MSG)

He is saying just because you can have sexual relations does not mean it is always spiritually right for you. Just because you can, does not mean you should.

He continues, if you went around doing whatever you thought you could get away with, you would be a slave to your whims. The tendency for too many of us is to see just how close to the edge we walk without falling over. You ask how much sexual activity is enough. Is it kissing, holding hands? What is the legal requirement? Is it just intercourse? All that Paul is saying is be aware of the fact that we have a tendency, as human beings, to try and push the boundaries.

> **You know the old saying, first you eat to live and then you live to eat. It may be true that the body is only temporary. You know it's going to die, but that is no excuse for stuffing your body with food or indulging it with sex.**
> I Corinthians 6:13 (MSG)

You can go to the Chinese food buffet and try to eat your $17.95 worth of food, and that is perfectly legal, but it may not be very healthy. You can go and have sexual relations with as many people as you want. You may even feel like you get away with it, but it does not necessarily make it spiritually correct. In fact, that type of behaviour is extremely damaging to your spirit.

A young woman in my congregation came to me for support. She felt the pressure of her peers and the media to have sexual relations. She wanted to hold onto her virginity for marriage. I decided to share with her the significance of the blood covenant and suddenly the world's philosophy appeared more misguided to her, and she found strength to continue to remain obedient to God's will.

Our culture can be very confusing. For example, our prevailing value system empowers women to do whatever they want with their bodies. If you are carrying a baby and you do not want the baby, the decision is the woman's to make. Scripture is counter to modern culture.

> **Since the Master honors you with a body, honor him with your body.**
> I Corinthians 6:13 (MSG)

If you have committed your life to Christ, then you commit your whole life, mind and body. Your body is no longer your own. In fact, scripture tells us that we were bought with a price, the blood of

Jesus, and we need to honour God and our bodies. This is a radical concept you may not want to hear. You may want to feel like you can do what you want with your body. The principle here is you need to learn how to honour God with your body, starting by getting enough sleep and nutrition.

> God honoured the master's body by raising it from the grave and he will treat yours with the same resurrection power.
> I Corinthians 6:14 (MSG)

This is the crazy truth about Christianity. The body is really important to God. Why didn't he just say he would raise us from the dead as spirits? Why would he just raise us and let us zip through space, a puff of light and there goes another spirit? He is not going to raise us up from the dead as spirits. He is going to raise us in bodily form.

If we go back to Genesis 1, when he created humankind he said **"it was very good"**. God liked what he created, he was not about to do away with it. Your body is important to God. God gave you a body, and you are to treat it with the same dignity as he does. Paul further explains how God values the human body in these terms, **"until that time…the time when we have been resurrected… remember that your bodies are created with the same dignity as the Master's body. You wouldn't take the Master's body off to a whorehouse, would you? I should hope not."** Paul continues, **"There's more to sex than mere skin on skin. Sex is as much a spiritual mystery as a physical act."** I Corinthians 6:16 (MSG).

Paul's statement provides us with the missing link in our relationships, the spiritual mystery surrounding our sexuality as human beings. We keep thinking it is purely physical. Sex is not purely physical; it is attached, in God's world, to being very spiritual. When you come together in sexual union the Bible says that two become one. We become one flesh.

> Since we want to become spiritually one with the Master, we must not pursue the kind of sex that avoids

commitment and intimacy, leaving us more lonely than ever—the kind of sex that can never become one.
I Corinthians 6:17 (MSG)

Here's God's design for healthy sexuality. We want to become spiritually one with the master. The goal as believers, as Christians and Christ followers, is to become like Christ.

Sex unites us in the spirit world with each other and with God.

Multiple relationships only leave us lonelier than ever. They allow us to avoid commitment and intimacy. We need to achieve commitment and intimacy for the sexual and spiritual union God intended. So many people are purposely avoiding commitment and intimacy. Young people are being encouraged to just get together for casual sex. In some relationships, the main purpose in becoming friends is for easy sex; having a sex buddy. Why are more and more people having this kind of relationship? Could it be that we are becoming more adverse to commitment and frightened of intimacy? As we avoid commitment and intimacy with each other, we empty ourselves of the capacity to experience commitment and intimacy with God. It becomes safer humanly, we believe, to be detached. The world is full of very lonely people.

Paul explains what he is talking about. **"There is a sense in which sexual sins are different from all others."** Why is that Paul? **"In sexual sin, we violate the sacredness of our own bodies."** What do you mean by that Paul? **"These bodies were made for God-given and God-modeled love, for 'becoming one' with another."**
I Corinthians 6:18 (MSG)

Why did God separate the *maleness* and the *femaleness* from that first creation Adam? So we could experience the oneness with each other that God experiences; so that we could experience the intense pleasure and joy that God experiences when he creates; so that we could have fun together as God has fun and that we could honour our bodies that God created as the temple of his presence on earth. We have taken that design and messed with it. Paul continues:

> **Or didn't you realize that your body is a sacred place, the place of the Holy Spirit? Don't you see that you can't live however you please; squandering what God paid such a high price for?**
> I Corinthians 6:20 (MSG)

I came to my relationship with Eileen as a fractured human being. As I shared earlier, my first attempt at commitment to Eileen did not include my body. I recall how many times in my life I said, "I love you God, but don't touch my body. I'll do with my body what I want. I will serve you with my mind and my emotions, but not with my body." What a crock!!!

Here's an example. You are in a relationship with someone who has a beautiful new, black, shiny jeep sitting in their driveway. You say to that person, "I really love you". Then you walk out of the house, take your key and scrape it down the side of their black jeep. Your actions say, "I just love you but not your possessions." What? Do you love or not love that person? If you love the person will you not cherish the things that they cherish? Will you not respect the things that they care about? We say to God, "I love you God, but ya know what, I will do with my body what I darn well please." The physical part of you is not some piece of property belonging to the spiritual part of you.

God owns the whole works, so let people see God in you.
I Corinthians 6:20 (MSG)

A very personal reflection.

The effect these verses had on me was that I was broken-hearted, sad, sorrowful and deeply regretful. I have used my body in ways that do not honour God. I have used my body in ways that are no reflection of God's love, beauty or glory and I want to let you know that in doing that, it absolutely broke my heart. I tested Eileen's love and trust. Some days, we still pay the price as a couple for some of the residual insecurities that our relationship had at the start. Some days old patterns of thinking creep in and I have to remind myself that God has forgiven me and I need to be responding from the new Spirit he has given me. I choose daily to walk in the freedom Jesus paid for me.

Many years ago, Eileen and I talked about how we damaged our bodies. We had experienced a seminar on relationships taught by Lorne Shepherd, in his association with the 100 Huntley Street organization. We sat together, on the side of our bed, holding hands and as best we could, called to mind the people with whom we had sexual relationships that were not in the safety and confines of a marriage. We just prayed for each one of them and asked God to unhook us from that person, to set our spirit free from the unhealthy bonds and the spiritual fragmentation left behind from those inappropriate relationships. We asked God to bring someone into their life to be the safe male and female we had not been. We just let God's beautiful healing grace flow over the fractured part of our lives.

Something amazing happened to me that night. I had nurtured a love-hate relationship with women; love them, need them, want them. But I hated the power and control they had over me, and hated myself for wanting them so badly. That anger developed into a core part of my personality. You could call me an angry man. I did not want to be angry! Anger just flowed at the most inappropriate times for a father, husband, pastor and Christian.

As Eileen and I prayed to be released from the spiritual damage done from our sexual past, God's peace washed over me, releasing pent up hurt, disappointment, insecurity, and spiritual pain. The giant source of anger flowed out from my body. I became a different man. God's healing spirit had done his work. God's shed blood had purchased my freedom. I finally experienced the verse I had read about for so long: **"So if the Son sets you free, you will be free indeed"** (John 8:36). I still get angry and have responses that are at times inappropriate. I am learning, with the continued help of the Holy Spirit, to capture each thought before it turns into an ugly response. But the core of my anger is gone…gone…gone!

God can do that, as broken as you may be.

In one of my most requested speaking series, *Healing the Spirit of Divorce*, I encourage listeners to pray and invite God to release them from the spiritual bonds created in the severed union as husband and wife. I also suggest they ask God to forgive them for violating the marriage covenant. I suggest you do the same; even if the marriage break-up was not your fault and not what you intended. If you have re-married it is important that you do this exercise before God, so that your spirit is free to bond without clutter. For those of you who have been sexually active outside of the marriage covenant, that covenant bonds you to each other. This bond, this spiritual union, must be broken, and healing must occur, before you will have an opportunity to create a relationship that lasts and honours God.

You must make a commitment to honour your body as God honours your body. To honour your body is to honour God. If you love God, you will love his stuff!

The Relationship Depot

Review

Sex has a place in God's design, much different though than the world's use of sex. This is where the unity, the coming together as one flesh, is honoured. The marriage covenant, like other covenants, is sealed by the spilling of blood.

God's way of sealing a deal was with blood. Marriage is sacred and saving your virginity allows the covenant to be sealed with blood.

The ultimate covenant relationship is Christ and his church with the shedding of blood on the cross. Your sexuality is the binding act for your marriage covenant with sexual intercourse re-enacting the original agreement. The sexual union is a reflection of God's unity with himself – Father, Son and Holy Spirit.

Sex is also the way to creation.

Understanding God's intention helps to sort through the confusion of sexual practices we see in the world today. Sex is rooted in self-satisfaction in the world's use, but God's roots are divine oneness and there is only one way there; building intimacy through the stages.

Biblical Instructions

> When Moses went and told the people all the LORD's words and laws, they responded with one voice, "Everything the LORD has said we will do." 4 Moses then wrote down everything the LORD had said. He got up early the next morning and built an altar at the foot of the mountain and set up twelve stone pillars representing the twelve tribes of Israel. 5 Then he sent young Israelite men, and they offered burnt offerings and sacrificed young bulls as fellowship offerings to the LORD. 6 Mo-

ses took half of the blood and put it in bowls, and the other half he splashed against the altar. 7 Then he took the Book of the Covenant and read it to the people. They responded, "We will do everything the LORD has said; we will obey." 8 Moses then took the blood, sprinkled it on the people and said, "This is the blood of the covenant that the LORD has made with you in accordance with all these words."

Exodus 24:3-8

For you know that it was not with perishable things such as silver or gold that you were redeemed from the empty way of life handed down to you from your ancestors, 19 but with the precious blood of Christ, a lamb without blemish or defect.

1 Peter 1:18-19

You say, "Food for the stomach and the stomach for food, and God will destroy them both." The body, however, is not meant for sexual immorality but for the Lord, and the Lord for the body.

I Corinthians 6:13

There's more to sex than mere skin on skin. Sex is as much spiritual mystery as physical fact. As written in Scripture, "The two become one." Since we want to become spiritually one with the Master, we must not pursue the kind of sex that avoids commitment and intimacy, leaving us more lonely than ever—the kind of sex that can never "become one." There is a sense in which sexual sins are different from all others. In sexual sin we violate the sacredness of our own bodies, these bodies that were made for God-given and God-modeled love, for "becoming one" with another. Or didn't you realize that your body is a sacred place, the place of the Holy Spirit? Don't you see that you can't live however you please, squandering what God paid such a high price for? The physical part of you is not some piece of property belonging to the spiritual part of you. God owns the whole works. So let people see God in and through your body.

I Corinthians 6:16-20

Building activities:

1. Write out your initial thoughts after reading about the blood covenant ritual.

Aisle Three | Sign the Contract; Seal the Deal

2. List any action you need to take in order to bring yourself in alignment with honouring covenants you have made or are preparing to make.

3. List any feelings or whims that you have become a slave to in your life.

4. Where have you pushed the boundaries in your behaviours? What did you feel? Regret? Anger? Disappointment?

The Relationship Depot

5. What do you see happening around you that pressures people to break their blood covenant?

Aisle Four
Take it to the Junk Yard

As I walked through the door of the cottage my senses were completely overwhelmed. Floor to ceiling, ceiling to floor, was completely covered in junk. Well, at least most of it looked like junk to me. There were broken canoe paddles, mildewed life preservers, old rope, newspapers stacked in bundles, sea shells and cardboard boxes piled high upon more cardboard boxes. My friends were in this cottage somewhere, but I sure could not see them with all the clutter and junk in the room. Eventually I spotted my friend Bill and his wife, Susie, sitting at their table at the other end of the living room. The table was piled high with old sailing magazines that barely left enough room for their coffee mugs.

There are many relationships, that when you start to examine them, look very similar to Bill and Susie's cottage. There are two people involved somewhere, but most of their relationship is occupied by unnecessary junk that takes up valuable emotional space.

I wonder how much space in your mind is occupied by unnecessary emotional clutter: bitterness, unforgiveness, old wounds, scars, hurts, painful memories, negative patterns of thinking and behaving. These all use up far more energy to sustain than positive attitudes. On a daily basis your mind is responsible for keeping all these unnecessary emotions functioning. Sustaining this junkyard consumes a great deal of mental energy that is not available to respond in healthy ways to your spouse, children or friends.

Think about this - the Bible teaches that we were made in the image of God (Genesis 1:27), and God is a God of order. The entire universe hangs together on specific principles like gravity, relativity, time and seasons. We were made to respond to an ordered world. We were also created to respond to emotional order, which produces healthy decisions and healthy relationships.

Our minds dislike being filled with emotional junk. Have you ever wondered why the fastest growing category of illness is mental illness? Depression is on the rise. The suicide rate is off the charts, and the divorce rate has now reached epidemic proportions. The straightforward answer to the question is that we are all carrying too much emotional junk. Your mind is constantly seeking the people or situations that will allow you to continue being hurt or rejected, or creating bitterness, sadness, disappointment, wounds, or anger.

The junk in your mind does not exist in a vacuum either. You feed the junk and prolong its existence. In fact, the junk is so powerful that it demands to be fed and it will pursue what it needs, with or without your conscious knowledge. Mental junk is so addictive that it will find ways to keep itself alive, even if it has to go underground to function.

Aisle Four | Take it to the Junk Yard

Regina's Story

When Regina, a member of my congregation, came to share her excitement about a new relationship with a good Christian man, I was thrilled for her. Her first marriage had ended when her husband, an abusive alcoholic, refused to repent. Regina had vowed after her divorce to never even date a man who touched alcohol in any way. To listen to Regina tell the story, her vow had paid off. She and George had been dating for months. They went to church together. They also made a vow of celibacy so that their bodies would honour God, and George did not drink alcohol. He had proposed to her and she was now in my office to ask me if I would marry them. It all looked good to me.

On a sunny Saturday in June, Regina and George tied the knot and headed out to a wilderness cottage in Northern Ontario for their honeymoon to live happily ever after. Unfortunately, that was not to be so. By the end of their first year of marriage, Regina was in my office again. Her excitement for her new relationship had been replaced with dread.

"This is totally unbelievable," she said to me, "George has started drinking." George's drinking escalated and sure enough, as if on some secret cue, George became abusive. Regina had to leave George for her safety. God would never require his children to remain in an unsafe environment.

Regina's story is not one that exists in isolation. All across this land, men and women are getting into relationships that look good on the surface, but turn out to be a mirror image of a previous relationship. Some reports put the divorce rate for second marriages as high as

The Relationship Depot

80%. Why do you think that is? After a first marriage and subsequent divorce, you would assume people have figured out how to do this relationship thing, right? As soon as the initial 'honeymoon' period is over, the time where people have been on their best emotional behaviour, the subconscious junk begins to take over and demands to be fed. The majority of people who are in a second or third relationship have never spent the time, energy and effort to clean out their emotional junk yard before starting another relationship, and instead of sorting through their junk, they leave yet another relationship. Regina and George will need to face their junk together, the same junk that needed to be dealt with in the first relationships.

Here is a truth you can ask God to help you comprehend, because that emotional junk has its own agenda.

If you do not deal with your junk, the junk will deal with you.

The statement above is as much a law of the universe as is gravity. It is impossible to escape the law of gravity and its effects when you are on this earth, and the same goes for the law of emotions. Emotions have the power to direct our behaviour.

Go back and read the bolded statement above. Did you do it? You will not find a way around this truth. God designed our brains to dislike holding onto unnecessary emotional garbage. To carry this unnecessary junk is to carry an emotional disease that will destroy your relationship and eventually destroy you. The goal of emotional pain, junk, garbage, or whatever you want to label it, is to destroy happiness, peace, fulfillment, satisfaction, intimacy, and rest.

Aisle Four | Take it to the Junk Yard

> Do not be anxious about anything, but in everything, by prayer and petition with thanksgiving present your requests to God. And the peace of God which transcends all understanding will guard your heart and minds in Christ Jesus.
> Philippians 4:6-7

Paul is sharing some amazing truths in these verses of scripture. The first is that we were never designed to hold onto, carry, store, or retain any form of mental or emotional anxiety. That is why Paul writes that we are not to be anxious. Anxiety in the human brain is emotional junk. Anxiety in the human brain is like sand in a car transmission, or water in a car's gas tank. Nothing works right with junk in it. Not your car, or your brain.

Paul wants to guard our hearts and minds, but from what? Emotional junk! Emotional junk distorts our earthly relationships and spiritual relationships. Emotional junk disconnects us from God and each other.

Emotional junk is the cancer of relationships.

Here are two big ideas:
1. When we carry excess emotional junk, our relationship with God becomes distant and disconnected.
2. When we carry excess emotional junk, our relationships with each other become distant and disconnected.

I have discovered in my own life, in my marriage, in my ministry and in my relationship with God that when I feel distant from Eileen I can usually track the source of those feelings to some unresolved issue. But here is an amazing revelation that I have come to understand. As I become more distant in my relationship with Eileen, I also become more distant in my relationship with God. And guess what? When I fail to deal with my God issues, and a spiritual distance sets in between God and me, so goes my relationship with Eileen...distant, detached, and growing colder by the day. Emotional junk is the cancer of relationships, both earthly and heavenly.

Relationships are important to God.

From the very beginning of time, God has always functioned in relationship; in relationship as the Godhead or the Trinity of Father, Son and Holy Spirit, in the relationship of Adam to the animal world and in the relationship with Adam and Eve. In God's own words, **"it is not good for man to be alone"** (Genesis 2:18). God desires us to be in a relationship with him. Jesus Christ was sent to earth to die so that all barriers of sin (spiritual junk) would be removed for a clear and direct relationship with him.

One of God's great relationship initiatives is the Church, his body. It was designed so that people from every tribe and nation, every walk of life, every background and experience could come together in unity of relationship, with Jesus Christ as its leader, to display to the world the unifying force of God's love. God also desires us to be in relationship with one another as families, friends, husbands and wives.

The character of God can be seen in a healthy earthly relationship.

The purpose of an earthly relationship is to be a reflection of God. When our relationships function well, they become an earthly reflection of God's divine nature. The character of God can be seen in a healthy earthly relationship. Think about some of the qualities we desire in our relationships; love, acceptance, understanding, purpose, closeness, trust, intimacy, and creativity. All of these qualities are found in God. They are found in God's relationship with himself as Father, Son and Holy Spirit. They are found in God's relationship to us by faith as he, the Holy Spirit, comes to dwell within us as humans.

The scripture teaches that we are sons and daughters of God (Galatians 6:4). When we enter into an earthly relationship, the highest purpose of that relationship is being a reflection of who God is. It seems to me that many of us have missed that 'higher' purpose for our relationships.

Just think of what would change in your life, or your family's life, or the life of your church, if we each agreed that we would work at making our earthly relationships a reflection of who God is. Just think of how different your current marriage relationship would be if you both made a commitment to build a relationship for the highest purpose; to be a reflection of who God is here on earth rather than self-fulfillment or pleasure. Would you yell as much? Would you sulk? Would you demand attention and seek to get your own way? Would you continue to engage in emotional blackmail? Would you withhold affection, sex or love to prove a point or get your own way?

The Relationship Depot

Here are a few tough questions for you to answer. Have courage and be honest. Is the current state of your relationships an authentic reflection of who God is? In other words, when people look at you and the relationships you are engaged in, do they see an accurate reflection of God? What image of God would someone get from examining your relationship? Would they see peace, love, unity, cooperation, collaboration, goodness, patience, self-control? Would they want to come to know the God who is reflected in your relationship, or would they prefer to run and hide from him.

When you refuse to address the junk, you carry and bring this junk to your relationships and essentially make a deliberate choice to damage the image of God. When you hold onto past hurts and wounds, when you allow pride to dominate and self to be in charge, you are sealing the fate of every relationship you enter to be less than fulfilling.

I guess the big question is whether or not you will choose to deal with your junk before you damage any further the relationship you are currently in, or move into new relationships. Ultimately, to choose a new attitude about relationships means elevating their purpose so that all of your relationships mirror God on earth.

I remember when my wife Eileen and I moved into our first apartment together. There was no way two apartments full of stuff were going to fit into one. Between us we had two couches, multiple side chairs, two sets of dishes, beds, dressers, a piano and organ, a big stereo system, and televisions. Some things had to go if we were going to live together. We began a process of sorting through our stuff and making decisions about what was important to each of us, and

Aisle Four | Take it to the Junk Yard

what would be important to both of us. As you can imagine, there were some tense moments as we each attempted to help the other person see the value in some item that they wished to keep. I am just not into Laredo figurines, especially when they are taking up valuable space for my record collection.

The sorting of physical stuff can be similar to the sorting of emotional stuff when two people form a relationship. There is simply not enough emotional space in a relationship for both couples to retain all their emotional junk. There is not enough 'room' in a relationship for each person to hold onto every piece of psychic pain that is housed in their brains. For a relationship to be healthy and succeed long-term both partners need to clean their emotional house.

If you are not yet in a relationship, there is no need to wait. Go ahead and begin this process. The sooner you submit your obedience and growth to God, the sooner the emotional junk will find its way into the dumpster, and the more likely you will be able to choose a person who is also emotionally healthy. Why is that? As you read earlier about Regina, we all make decisions driven by our emotional junk. We are wired with emotional radar that is self-attracting.

The other day, one of our neighbour's children returned to their family home for a visit. It was quite startling to see the young, gangly, awkward teenager, who had left home to pursue university, return home as a beautiful and confident woman with a masters degree. Here is the really fascinating part about our short visit. In conversation she sounded just like her mother! She had the same vocal inflections, the same vowel distinctiveness, and the same rise of voice at the end of her phrases. But she also had her father's mannerism of standing with her hand on her hip while she was contemplating what she would say next.

Sociologists tell us that we inherit far more than physical mannerisms from our parents; we pick up political ideologies and values as well. How we view the world is filtered though our parents' beliefs and values. We also develop patterns of thinking and responding, in many cases that are identical to what we experienced at home. Some of those behaviours we disliked and we vowed never to respond or behave like that. Many more never register in our conscious thoughts.

There is always some distortion when a value, good or bad, healthy or unhealthy, is passed down through to the next generation. My brain took the values of a stoic European-style household and translated it into behaviours that were aloof and lacking intimacy. Perhaps, if there had been other children in the house they may have filtered those values differently. But parental values, what you see in your growing up life, what you experience at the hands or voices of your parents will get filtered, to some degree either positively or negatively.

Those values get filtered by your own temperament, how God has wired you, your emotional capacity and intellect. This is why my twin daughters are quite different in how they process material and what values they have adopted, even though they grew up in the same household at the identical time. So many of your primary response mechanisms like anger, avoidance, confrontation, withdrawal, acceptance, understanding and tolerance have been adapted from your family of origin. Some of your responses are rooted in your

Aisle Four | Take it to the Junk Yard

sinful nature; sin, in this instance, being defined as 'the right to myself'. Regardless of how or where you developed your patterns of responding, you and you alone are responsible for them and need to accept responsibility.

The Bible speaks about this process of passing along patterns of sinful behaviour from generation to generation. Here, Moses is making two more stone tablets to replace the ones that were broken in pieces when the people of Israel did not want to adhere to the Ten Commandments. Pay close attention to the time frame in which God operates.

> **He punishes the children and their children for the sin of the parents to the third and fourth generation.**
> Exodus 34:7b

God is clearly expressing that sinful behaviours and responses have a shelf-life of three or four generations. In other words, it can take three to four generations to work these sinful patterns out of an extended family's life. Take a moment to think back through the generations of your family. Can you see any patterns of behaviour that emerge? Is there a line of divorce through the generations; addiction to alcohol, drugs, sex, gambling, poverty, anger issues, abuse, failure, avoiding issues, making peace at any cost, the need to earn approval, a crisis of self-esteem, constant anxiety, illegal behaviours, perhaps depression or even suicide?

Do not despair, God is faithful. Our creator always has a solution to the sin that causes emotional junk. Read David's prayer.

> Do not hold against us the sins of past generations; may your mercy come quickly to meet us, for we are in desperate need.
> Psalm 79:8

Does that statement reflect you today? Are you in desperate need? Do you need God to break the chains of generational sin, the stinking thinking and emotional junk in your life and the life of your family? Then pray, as David prayed, and say to God, do not hold against us the sins of the fathers; may your mercy come quickly to meet us, for we are in desperate need. Recall what we read earlier in Exodus 34, that **"the Lord is loyal in love for a thousand generations, forgiving iniquity, rebellion, and sin."**

> **Know therefore that the LORD your God is God; he is the faithful God, keeping his covenant of love to a thousand generations of those who love him and keep his commands.**
> Deuteronomy 7:9

God is faithful to forgive sin when we invite him to do so. When we break the patterns of generational sin that we have adopted, God then declares his mercy and love will flow to a thousand generations. When you deal with your junk, you can pass along these new ways of thinking to your children, your children's children, your great-grandchildren, your great-great-grandchildren and their children. Is that not motivation enough to get honest, do some hard thinking, and some praying? The effort is well worth it, God desires it, and our children need it.

Aisle Four | Take it to the Junk Yard

Alex's story

"She's angry all the time. When we met, she was the sweetest woman I ever knew". This is what Alex, a 36 year old man, recently married for the second time, shared with me in desperation. His wife Anna constantly criticizes him and at times gets so angry she is yelling at him. "I'm walking on eggshells all the time," he confided to me.

Alex and Anna also live with her two children from her previous marriage. Alex told me that he grew up in a family where his mother stayed home and managed the household and children, while his father worked in the local plant. He also confided that his mother was the rule maker and enforcer.

"Although my mother was always home, I tried to avoid her," he told me. "The minute I walked in the door, she was criticizing me. But it was confusing because after a while she would calm down and want to share her day with me."

Alex, like you, has this emotional junk that he drags everywhere. The originator of all that junk is his family of origin.

Alex was confused and defeated when his mother was criticizing. God knows that words are powerful, that is why he tells you to watch what comes out of your mouth. Make it words that build the other up (Colossians 3:8; James 3:10).

An unhealed emotional wound is like a cut that never gets cleaned, but is stitched up anyways. The cut gets infected and then needs to be reopened again to let the pus out. It still needs to be cleaned and protected to heal over. Otherwise, the unhealed wound can create an even bigger problem. Since Alex did not get to tell his mother how her criticizing defeated him, he carried that wound in his junk yard. These wounds went from relationship to relationship. The core of those wounds is how others abused you – emotionally, physically and spiritually. Alex was abused emotionally by being criticized and continually told he was less than enough, and he was taught to be afraid of being vulnerable.

Alex is now in a second marriage, which is very much like his first one. He married a critical and judgemental woman. How could he make the same choice twice? Alex is now realizing he is marrying women who are just like his mother, the mother he tried to avoid. There is a generational sinful pattern of behaviour that Alex needs help to unmask. He needs to come to grips with the issues of being vulnerable and his own need to be involved with critical women.

Alex has committed to ask God for His wisdom to unmask the illusions and lies perpetrated on his life by the sinful words of his mother. He is committed to asking God to help him understand the confusing pattern of pushing away and then seeking closeness. At some point in his journey, he will need to ask God to help him understand his mother's behaviour and recognize what emotions are driving his behaviours.

Alex may then come to see his mother in a new light and understand the generational sin that his mother is carrying and continues to perpetrate on the family. He can then ask God to replace his fear of rejection with his assurance of love.
Together, we examined how he felt about God as Father. We

Aisle Four | Take it to the Junk Yard

explored a few questions that might reveal deep beliefs that hold the pattern in place. Does he think God is unreliable, like his mother was unreliable? Does he feel that God disapproves of him all the time? Until Alex resolves unhealed wounds inflicted by his mother, he may struggle to really trust God.

I sent Alex away to read and even memorize the 139th Psalm. Through this psalm, he will come to learn of God's great love and compassion for him and that God has a plan for him, in spite of his pain. As Alex resolves his pattern, seeks forgiveness and commits to living a Godly life, he can rest assured that the generational curse that he grew up under will be broken. As he gains confidence in his own spiritual health, he can then begin a confident dialogue with Anna about her criticism.

Only God can heal a wounded spirit, a broken heart, or a junk-filled mind.

I took the opportunity to help my congregation to start cleaning out their junk yard. As everyone arrived at church on Sunday morning, they were greeted with a dumpster placed right outside the front doors of the church. Emblazoned on the side of the dumpster was the word JUNK. As they walked through the front entrance on their way to the auditorium there were numerous piles of scrap wood about 2 feet in length. During the Sunday service, I spoke about the necessity to get rid of the junk yard in our mind and allow God to heal the wounds and brokenness we have collected from our time here on earth. At the end of the service, each person was invited to pick a piece of wood from the pile and take a marker to write on the scrap wood the issues they desire God to heal in their lives. As

The Relationship Depot

they left the auditorium that morning, they tossed their junk piece of wood into the back of the dumpster. The dumpster represented the Almighty God who takes our junk and disposes of it in his landfill site, never to be seen again. (Isaiah 1:18)

I want to encourage you to create a visual symbol that you can use to hand your emotional junk over to God. It may be as simple as a sheet of paper where you write down what God shows you throughout this process and then shred it at the end. You may prefer to burn the paper, or even write on a piece of scrap wood and then throw it in the garbage or fire. Balloons are another way to eliminate mental junk. Write what you want to send off to God, and release it outside.

There are many ways to symbolize cleaning out junk that gets stuck hanging around too long. One evening, after a very difficult period in my daughter's life, I took her up the side of a high cliff. We carried with us a collection of odd cups, saucers and mugs. She assigned to each piece of china an issue to give over to God. Picking up each item she threw each one off the cliff with a loud yell. We laughed heartily as we heard the cups and saucers smash against the side of the cliff, knowing that the power of God had shattered the power of these hungry issues in her life.

There is something potent about physically acting on your mental decisions. Much like writing out a goal propels you toward it, writing out your emotional junk can help distance you from it.

The second amazing truth is that God has a sure fire way to help us get rid of our emotional junk. According to Paul's writing in Philippians 4:6-7 we are to pray...look at it..."**about everything**".

Aisle Four | Take it to the Junk Yard

You must learn to pray first and think second. That's right! Pray first, before you start to problem solve and look for solutions. Go straight to the top, right from the start. Talk to God at the first sign of emotional distress. Do not wait. Do not debate. Talk to God! Petition him. Thank him for your life and circumstances. Invite him to join you in your situation.

Paul says this communication with God is the very first step to experiencing a peace which defies explanation, or in Paul's words, "transcends understanding". Notice that he says this peace will "guard your heart and *minds (italics* added) in Christ Jesus".

When we pray first and think second, God's peace becomes the guardian of our hearts, the root of our emotions and minds, where emotional and cognitive stability is based.

Here is a prayer you can use every day on this journey towards a healthy relationship with God and others:

> **Search me O God, and know my heart; test me and know my anxious thoughts. See if there is any offensive way in me, and lead me in the way everlasting.**
> Psalm 139: 23-24

David begins by giving God permission to *search him.* Can you imagine the power of God searching the deepest recess of your heart and mind? Nothing in you can be hidden from his light and love. Even the issues that you have buried deep in your subconscious mind are subject to God's searching. Allow God to bring out of the darkness the shame you carry.

David asks God to *know his heart.* This statement is very important.

The Relationship Depot

Over the years, I have been very disappointed in my own actions. My behaviour in my relationships has definitely not been a reflection of who God is, yet I do love the Lord with all my heart. David is saying to God, in effect, "please do not judge just my actions, check out my heart...I know it is oriented in the right direction".

David's request to God to search out his heart, and the frustration he expresses that some of his actions are not quite lining up with his heart's desire, is echoed by Paul.

> I know that good itself does not dwell in me, that is, in my sinful nature. For I have the desire to do what is good, but I cannot carry it out. For I do not do the good I want to do; but the evil I do not want to do - this I keep on doing.
> Romans 7:18-19

Eugene Peterson's translation in *The Message* expresses the same verses this way:

> But I need something more! For if I know the law but still can't keep it, and if the power of sin within me keeps sabotaging my best intentions, I obviously need help! I realize that I don't have what it takes. I can will it, but I can't do it. I decide to do good, but I don't really do it; I decide not to do bad, but then I do it anyway.
>
> My decisions, such as they are, don't result in actions. Something has gone wrong deep within me and gets the better of me every time.

Wow, these verses of scripture sound like they are a description of me! Could they be an accurate reflection of your behaviours? Notice

Aisle Four | Take it to the Junk Yard

the call to God for help and the acknowledgement of the false power behind sin.

"I obviously need help! Something has gone wrong deep within me and gets the better of me every time." These words are an accurate description of so many people who have failed to let God deal with their emotional junk. They may have, at some time in their lives, made a commitment of their life to Christ or been born again, or raised their hand in a church service, or walked down an aisle in response to an altar call, or asked God to forgive their sin, but have failed to progress any further in their spiritual development.

The original sin that separates them from God has been forgiven, but they have never dealt with the scars of that original sin which play out every day in their attitudes, actions and behaviours.

Christians who fall into this category are very similar to what is called, in the world of addictions, a 'dry drunk'. Dry drunks do not drink alcohol any more but their behaviours, attitudes and actions continue to be the same, unchanged even though they no longer drink. There are Christians who make what we call a "profession of faith in Christ" but never allow God's Spirit access to their inner self through their attitudes, actions and behaviours. They never make a full commitment to trust and offer obedience.

Paul, in Ephesians, chapter 4, refers to this type of believer. Let's call them a "dry believer" because they are making choices from their old nature or old self, rather than making choices from the new self that has been renewed by the Spirit of God.

David understood that he was powerless to change his life without the direct intervention of God. He understood that positive thinking was not enough on its own. Even will power, goal setting or accountability partners are not enough on their own. Something greater is needed. A higher power is needed, and that higher power is the Holy Spirit of God, who can transform and renew our inner self, who can clean up the junk in our mind...*if we give him permission to do so.*

David says search me; know my heart and now test me. David is asking God to show him what he is really made of. He is asking God to test his heart, to check it out, to give him a status report, to take his spiritual temperature and find out where his anxieties lie.

You need God to do the testing and checking and searching in your life, because you will never be truthful with yourself. That's right! You have been so corrupted by sin (the desire to run your own life) that even when you ask yourself for the truth, you don't really want to know the truthful answer. You are just like a little kid who asks another kid what they really think about you, but you don't really want to know the truth. So you must ask God to do the searching and the testing because God is reliable and will always give you the truth about yourself.

God is reliable and will always give you the truth about yourself.

Remember that the junk in your mind will do anything to keep itself alive. Your emotional junkyard has no desire to be well; it has no desire to die and let the healthy you live. Your emotional junkyard is committed to its ongoing survival. So get this - if you ask *your Self* to get rid of *your* junk what do you think will happen? *You* will hand

Aisle Four | Take it to the Junk Yard

over some token junk, just enough to think you are getting well, just enough to give you the illusion of progress, just enough to satisfy *your Self* that you have complied with its wishes. But you will give *your Self* no more than the minimum required to get you off its back.

In talking about these issues years ago with my father, he made the following statement "self will never cast out self". I was a teenager at that time and I have never forgotten what my father shared. Let me express that statement in the terms we are using - "junk will never get rid of junk". Asking your own self, your own power, to get rid of the emotional junk that now is defining your life is like asking the fox to guard the hen house. In spiritual terms, we are saying that sin will not cast out or deal with sin.

The *Self* will limit you to improve itself only so far. To be truly well, both emotionally and spiritually, you need the intervention of the Spirit of God in your life. He alone is your source of truth.

David invited God to be his searchlight into the deepest recesses of his heart and mind. He invited God to test him to find out where his anxieties were hidden. This concept of hidden anxieties is very important to us because most of our negative junkyard behaviours are rooted in some form of fear, which produces anxiety. David invited God to bring to his awareness the hidden fears that drove his junkyard behaviours. He asked God to bring those fears out and into the light, knowing that it could turn out to be a challenging process to heal.

The power of a hidden fear is its ability to live in darkness. Once exposed, a fear can be seen for what it is - a shadow, a hollow truth without substance, a distortion of God's intention. In other words, a fear is a lie. When exposed to God's truth, fear dissolves and the lie is replaced with God's truth.

The power of hidden fear is in its ability to make us believe that we will die emotionally if the fear is exposed. Much like a child engaged in a temper tantrum, fear will make great emotional noise trying to get us to back off from exposing the real truth.

Fear is the root cause of all junkyard behaviour.

Fear is the root cause of dysfunctional relationships. The very first emotion recorded in the bible in Genesis (3:10) is fear. The moment Adam and Eve disobeyed God, the emotion of fear surfaced. Where there is obedience to God there is an absence of fear. Since God desires obedience from his children, he will do everything we ask to help us achieve that obedience and live a life without fear. Being his child, God desperately wants to help you become all you can be.

One of the reasons David could submit himself to the emotional and spiritual searching of a Holy God is because he understood that God made him and created him for a specific purpose.

Earlier in the 139th Psalm (13-16) David writes:

> For you created my inmost being; you knit me together in my mother's womb. I praise you because I am fearfully and wonderfully made; your works are wonderful, I know that full well.
>
> My frame was not hidden from you when I was made in the secret place. When I was woven together in the depths of the earth, your eyes saw my unformed body.

> All the days ordained for me were written in your book before one of them came to be.

Knowing that God oversaw his creation, and even designed a specific plan for his life, gave David courage to ask God to fix him. Who better to fix something that is broken than the one who made it in the first place? Who better to invite into your life to heal and restore than the very God who created you?

When you don't address early wounds you take them with you to all your relationships.

That's right, every single relationship. If you go from one relationship to the next trying to stay away from the hurt, the wounds start to accumulate. You carry the original wound, and all the new manifestations created from the relationships you try to escape in. That includes the relationships you had with your parents and siblings. Soon you have a junkyard.

When you get married and then divorce, the previous marriage comes along into the next relationship. All the fear, resentment or anger, that did not get cleaned up will come along too. Alex's response was to leave his first marriage without healing the original wound. He left his marriage because his wife was criticizing all the time; yet he married another critical woman. See the pattern?

There is absolutely no way to make a clean break from one relationship to the next. As we jump, trying to avoid the pain, the junk pile gets even higher, making it harder to find God underneath.

The Relationship Depot

Every relationship has a spiritual bond attached to it.

Every relationship has a spiritual bond attached to it. All your relationships get bonded in the spirit world. If you break a relationship, it gets ripped apart in the spirit world too. So what do you look like inside after all those broken relationships? Well, you look like you were at the butcher shop. Your spirit is fractured, torn and ripped apart. If you had multiple sexual relationships or a lot of in-depth emotional relationships, and you leave those, going on to the next person, then the next person doesn't see you coming all broken and emotionally bleeding. You bring that brokenness and try to bond with the next person, but the bond is not stable.

True intimacy cannot thrive when two unhealed wounds are present.

Relationships only adhere permanently to other relationships that have been properly prepared and are devoid of emotional grease, dust, pain or simply emotional junk. You need to prepare for a new relationship, a healthy relationship.

Here is how Jesus explained this concept to his disciples.

> No one sews a patch of unshrunk cloth on an old garment, for the patch will pull away from the garment, making the tear worse. Neither do men pour new wine into old wineskins. If they do, the skins will burst, the wine will run out and the wineskins will be ruined. No, they pour new wine into new wineskins, and both are preserved.
> Matthew 9:16-17

Aisle Four | Take it to the Junk Yard

Eugene Peterson, in *The Message*, translates the verses this way:

> **No one cuts up a fine silk scarf to patch old work clothes; you want fabrics that match. And you don't put your wine in cracked bottles.**

Cracked wine bottles! What an illustration Jesus gave about our lives together. We pour a new relationship into a cracked bottle; no wonder it does not last. It just drips out, until one day there is nothing left and we are left wondering what went wrong.

Jesus is calling you to clean out your junkyard. Clean that festering wound. Let go of dragging that junk with you everywhere. Unpack the sealed box. Do the preparation necessary to build a lasting relationship. Take the time. Break the generational curse. Plug the leaks in the bottle, or become a whole new bottle ready to be filled. Become relationally leak proof.

Getting rid of junk does not mean booting your spouse out and finding another, though. God is really clear about divorce.

> **Jesus replied, Moses permitted you to divorce your wives because your hearts were hard. But it was not this way from the beginning.**
> Matthew 19:8

God's intention is for you to honour the marriage covenant and grow within your relationship. Heal those old wounds with your spouse. You may even come to realize that your spouse is God's perfect person to keep you focused on your emotional junk and move you towards healing. When you avoid dealing with an old wound, an addiction is then created. Seeking relief, for the moment, from the 'fix' rather than asking God to heal the wound. Growth and spiritual maturity are created by healing those wounds; growth that God wants you to discover in your marriage relationship.

What you don't acknowledge, God cannot heal.

Truthfully, you pretty well don't stand a chance of having a healthy relationship if you have not dealt with your junkyard. The good news is that God can heal. He can restore your wounds, but you will need to own up. What you don't acknowledge, God cannot heal. If you want to hide it and follow what others are doing by having multiple relationships, or blame that failed marriage on the horrible person you were married to, then the junkyard continues to pile up.

Being married does not mean tolerating mistreatment from your spouse either. You absolutely get to mark your boundaries when they are hurting out at others. It is also an opportunity to act as Jesus would in the relationship, with kindness and compassion. In some situations you may need to separate to protect yourself or

to protect your spouse. You need to pray that your spouse will get reconnected with God. Then let God do his job. Step away, maintain healthy boundaries and let God do his job with your spouse, while you strengthen your own relationship with him.

> **Be kind and compassionate to one another, forgiving each, just as in Christ God forgave you.**
> Ephesians 4:32

Marriage is primarily spiritual, making you whole and healthy. Repairing is done at both a spiritual and human level. Start at the spiritual level, with God. There will be times in your relationship when you will suffer, but let the spirit of God work with you and you will become a reflection of the divine.

Are you ready to invite God of the universe, by his Holy Spirit, to come and clean out your emotional junk yard, expose your fears and lead you in a life-giving, life-affirming path?

Are you ready for THE relationship of your life? A relationship with God that is so deeply satisfying that you will never again ask a human being to be what only God can be and do for you. To have a relationship with God will complete you spiritually, so that you will be free to love another without strings, or emotional games.

Here is what God has pledged to you. First he has given you Jesus as your guarantee that a healthy spiritual life is possible. By the death of Jesus on the cross, and subsequent resurrection, God has demonstrated that the power of sin can be defeated. Second, God has given you this pledge of victory over sin and the emotional junkyard. This pledge is found in Philippians 4:13 where Paul writes:

I can do everything through him (Christ) who gives me strength.

Make a commitment to God, to yourself and to the people you love, to do the work necessary for cleaning out your emotional junkyard. God is standing by waiting to be invited into your life and situation. Why not invite him to come in right now? For those of us who believe we have blown it big time, and for those who may be scared to even try again, I offer you these words of hope from Paul, so that you know it is not too late, you are not too far gone, there is still hope.

The Relationship Depot

> And we know that in all things God works for the good of those who love him, who have been called according to his purpose.
> Romans 8:28

> For I am convinced that neither death nor life, neither angels nor demons, neither the present nor the future, nor any powers, neither height nor depth, nor anything else in all creation, will be able to separate us from the love of God that is in Christ Jesus our Lord.
> Romans 8:38-39

You are loved, there is hope and you can be whole, with God on your side.

Aisle Four | Take it to the Junk Yard

Review

The character of God can be seen in a healthy earthly relationship. A man and woman respecting each other, supporting and growing. We don't always arrive at marriage in good enough condition to fulfill that role. God is growing you in that direction. The accumulation of emotional junk in your system gets in the way of God's character shining through.

One of the reasons we avoid addressing our emotional junk is fear. Fear that shame and guilt will be to overwhelming to handle. The shame and guilt keeps it locked in place.

Yet we continue to be reminded of the freedom we will experience once clearing it all out. Scripture reminds us that Jesus died for our sins, the same sins we continue to burden ourselves with today.

God is working to get some emotional order in your life so obedience can be achieved and with obedience comes healthy decision-making and Godly relationships.

If you do not deal with your junk, the junk will deal with you.

The highest purpose of our relationship is a reflection of God.

You need God to do the testing and checking and searching because you will never be truthful with yourself, but God will.

Self will never cast out self – junk will never get rid of junk.

The power of a hidden fear is its ability to live in darkness – but exposed it's just a hollow truth, a distortion of God's intention.

Fear is the root cause of all junkyard behaviour.

The Relationship Depot

Biblical Instructions

> Do not be anxious about anything, but in every situation, by prayer and petition, with thanksgiving, present your requests to God. 7 And the peace of God, which transcends all understanding, will guard your hearts and your minds in Christ Jesus.

Philippians 4:6-7

> ...maintaining love to thousands, and forgiving wickedness, rebellion and sin. Yet he does not leave the guilty unpunished; he punishes the children and their children for the sin of the parents to the third and fourth generation.

Exodus 34:7b

> For I know that good itself does not dwell in me, that is, in my sinful nature.] For I have the desire to do what is good, but I cannot carry it out. 19 For I do not do the good I want to do, but the evil I do not want to do—this I keep on doing.

Romans 7:18-19

> No one sews a patch of unshrunk cloth on an old garment, for the patch will pull away from the garment, making the tear worse. 17 Neither do people pour new wine into old wineskins. If they do, the skins will burst; the wine will run out and the wineskins will be ruined.

No, they pour new wine into new wineskins, and both are preserved.

Matthew 9:16-17

Be kind and compassionate to one another, forgiving each other, just as in Christ God forgave you.

Ephesians 4:32

Building activities

1. What emotional junk are you feeding?

2. List the ways you could get rid of the junk.

The Relationship Depot

3. Who has been and is currently impacted by your junk?

4. Repeat these words in prayer:
Search me, God, and know my heart;
   test me and know my anxious thoughts.
See if there is any offensive way in me,
   and lead me in the way everlasting.
Psalm 139:23-24

Come back and write out what has been revealed to you.

5. What sin do you continue to repeat over and over again, even though you try everything to stop?

6. Take that sin to God in prayer.

7. Who is a trusted person you could confess this sin?

Aisle Five
Renovate and Redecorate

On an unusually hot spring Sunday morning, with the air conditioner in the auditorium working hard to keep the hundreds of church attendees comfortable, I walked onto the stage to present my sermon. Strapped to my back and over a freshly laundered white shirt, was a backpack weighing in at almost 60 pounds. I spoke for about 20 minutes before making any mention of the obviously heavy bag on my back. I was running out of steam. The sweat on my forehead was dripping into my eyes. I reached up and pushed the straps of the backpack off my shoulders. The contents, paving stones, hit the wooden stage floor with a very dull, but loud, thud. I was so happy to get that weight off my back and the audience was witness to the expression of relief that spread across my face. I was free of the burden of those paving stones, and I felt like I could dance across the stage. That was the moment I told the audience, "Forgiveness is like dropping this backpack and having the ability to move more freely again."

Every paving stone in that backpack represented a story of unforgiveness; an abusive parent, a controlling ex-spouse, a sexual assault, an embezzling relative, a mean teacher, and the list goes on. Life is full of situations where we get hurt, and over the years, we carry that hurt in our mind and in our spirit. Some of the pain we bury at the bottom of the backpack, out of sight, while other pain we carry near the top for easy access. We can easily bring it out and examine it, check it over and remind ourselves of the injustice. No matter where we carry the pain, it becomes heavier every passing year. Eventually that excess emotional and spiritual weight slows us down, makes us mentally tired, dries us up spiritually, and wears us out physically. We were never designed to carry unnecessary emotional, mental and spiritual stress. If we carry it long enough we get systemically sick in our spirits, minds and bodies.

Holding back on forgiveness in your spiritual and emotional life acts like cancer does in your physical life. It rots away at the vibrancy that once was you. Your zest for life, your joy and emotional stability are affected. It also rots away at your spiritual connection with God, leaving you feeling alone, unloved and, in some cases, angry. This spiritual depression, rooted in hopelessness, is fed by the un-forgiven wounds you carry with you every day.

Joan's Story

Joan insisted on seeing me at least twice a week, sometimes more. As a new pastor, I had not yet discovered the power of boundaries, and I recall saying to Joan that I saw more of her than I did of my wife. Joan wanted some help with a physical problem of advanced arthritis and persistent migraine headaches. Our sessions were primarily to talk about her relationship problems. As a child her father would punish her by locking her in the chicken coop. Memories of this frightening experience had many consequences, including a dislike of eating chicken. I was desperate to find an answer to Joan's issues. For weeks, she recounted the same stories of abuse and rejection and no suggestion from me, or direction from the word of God, seemed to be penetrating her thinking. Counseling day came again, and sure enough Joan was booked for an extended time.

In the few moments between my appointments I began to earnestly pray. "God show me how to help Joan. Give me wisdom, direction, anything," I cried.

Joan started the session with the same story of aches and pains. "Did you try any of the suggestions we agreed upon last week?" I queried.

And, of course, I got the same answer. "No, not really. I didn't think they would work; my life is just so messed up."

During Joan's distressing discourse I had an 'aha' moment. The Holy Spirit lit up my mind. "Joan," I began. "Have you heard the story in the Bible of the man sitting by the pool of Bethesda? The one where the first person entering the pool after an angel has stirred up the waters would be healed?"

"Yes," she answered. I opened my Bible and began to read.

> **Now there is in Jerusalem near the Sheep Gate a pool, which in Aramaic is called Bethesda and which is surrounded by five covered colonnades. Here a great number of disabled people used to lie; the blind, the lame, the paralyzed. One who was there had been an**

Aisle Five | Renovate and Redecorate

> invalid for thirty-eight years. When Jesus saw him lying there and learned that he had been in this condition for a long time, he asked him, "Do you want to get well?" "Sir," the invalid replied, "I have no one to help me into the pool when the water is stirred. While I am trying to get in, someone else goes down ahead of me." Then Jesus said to him, "Get up! Pick up your mat and walk." At once the man was cured; he picked up his mat and walked. The day on which this took place was a Sabbath"
> John 5:2-9

Here is this guy who has been sitting by a pool for 38 years, waiting to get well. Every time the angel of the Lord stirred the waters, he missed it. I do not know how he missed it. He had 38 years to get it right. He could have rigged some pulleys, paid someone to carry him, or sat so close to the edge that someone could have pushed him in. But for 38 long, agonizing years he missed the opportunity to get well. For whatever reason, he could not pull it off.

I raised my head out of my Bible and turned to Joan and posed the same question Jesus asked the man by the pool, "Do you want to get well?"

By the way, Joan was a brilliant woman. She was sharp, with an aptitude for numbers and math that is beyond my understanding. Joan sat back in her chair, and a long silence ensued. When she finally spoke, she revealed, in a voice so strong and clear, "No, I do not want to be well." Another silence.

"For two reasons," she announced. "One, I will lose my disability pension, and two, my children won't have a reason to come and visit

The Relationship Depot

me." I sat dumbfounded in front of her.

After hours upon hours of counselling over several months with no apparent progress, we had the answer. Joan had no real interest in getting better. She did not want to be well. She had a vested interest in not getting well. She just wanted to talk about getting well. She had no intention of doing any action that would take her away from the life she had defined for herself. Joan was a physically sick woman who had painful arthritis and migraine headaches that worked for her. That is the way Joan chose to define her life.

Most of us would think that's crazy, that she is nuts; who wouldn't want to be well if they could? The unfortunate answer is thousands. Thousands, maybe even millions, of people are walking about every day, carrying the effects of an illness in their life and ignoring Christ's opportunity to be well. Every week I meet the walking wounded in my office, at the coffee shop or at church on Sunday. For years they have had the opportunity to take responsibility for their own emotional and spiritual health, and for some reason, they have not done so. Now, they are sick, really sick. Their spirit has a gaping wound, their emotions are diseased, their thinking distorted. Their body beginning to fail, being eaten away daily by a completely curable disease, the cancer of the unforgiven.

During our Sunday evening service, Joan came up to the front of the church for prayer. The elders and pastors gathered around her and one of the elders placed a small drop of anointing oil on her forehead. It was my turn to pray. Joan asked for healing from her arthritis and her headaches. I was taught by my father to wait on the Lord for a few moments before praying for his wisdom to be revealed. I waited and then placed my hand on Joan's shoulder and began to pray. I prayed for God to give Joan the courage and the desire to seek forgiveness for those who had hurt her. Joan needed to be released from the power they still had over her, power she was giving them daily by her refusal to forgive. I then spoke directly to Joan and told her that as soon as she would start the process of forgiveness, she would experience freedom from her physical pain, as her arthritis and headaches were physical manifestations of what was happening to her emotionally and spiritually. Joan did not speak to me for weeks. Some years later, Joan died from her illnesses, alone.

I am going to ask you the same question Jesus asked of the man at the pool, and that I also asked Joan in my office: "Do you want to be well?"

In fact, if you listen very carefully, in your spirit, you may hear Jesus' voice asking you the same question.

Jesus always amazes me by his acts of compassion.

I am sure if it had been me passing by the man at the pool, I might have thought he was a loser. How stupid could he be not to figure out how to get well, after all those years? I might pass right by, maybe put a buck in his cup and think, he got what he deserved. Good thing Jesus is not me. Notice in the story that Jesus does not even ask him what he had been up to, or how he managed to waste the last 38 years. Jesus asked him one simple question. The answer changed the man's life forever. He simply asked if he wanted to be well.

The Relationship Depot

He could have also asked a few more poignant questions. Have you waited long enough? Have you suffered enough? Are you tired of the pain and frustration? Are you ready? Have you had your fill of anxiety, sleepless nights, and self-medication? Do you want to be well?

If you are hanging onto old issues, this question is for you too. How you answer will change everything. You are either going to move forward or remain the same. I hope you will keep moving forward and know the freedom of removing your backpack.

Bitterness and emotional pain stay alive by you feeding them.

Feeding the pain is when you take the abuse, verbal attack, resentful look, or critical words out of their hiding place in your heart and you...

NURSE IT

Here is what it sounds like: "Oh poor me. No one loves me. Everyone is so mean to me. She is so unkind. This hurts so much. I have never felt like this before. I am so wounded. Life is so unfair. I never had a chance. I will never get over this."

Next you...

CURSE IT

"That blankety-blank, son of a gun, (all expletives deleted...add your own), I will make him pay if it's the last thing I do. They won't get away with this." You may even take the person out of the little cage in your heart where you have them imprisoned and visualize yourself slapping them around a little before you stick them back in again. There now, did that not make you feel better? Then you begin to…

REHEARSE IT

Every detail of the encounter you dredge up from your memory; every detail, every sound and every word. You can see the expression on their faces, feel the sting of their words and hear painful phrases like;

"You're a bad boy."

"I don't love you anymore."

"I had an affair."

"You are stupid."

It is all there in your mind, in vivid colour and in surround sound, as you rehearse it over and over again. After all, you can never let this go. Without adequate acknowledgement, you feel it is necessary to hold onto this hurt. So you recall this memory over and over again. Before long, you begin to define your life by your pain.

Joan described herself as a victim, treated unfairly by her father, the very person who should have been her protector. Victims are everywhere; the news is full of them. Almost everybody you meet has been a victim of something. Victim is a 'hot' word in our world today. And if you are not a victim then maybe you are a survivor. That sounds like a much better word. Well-meaning people everywhere are turning their victimization into survivor-hood. Survivor has also become a 'hot' word.

The Bible says we are to define our lives as VICTORS.

To me, a survivor is a victim turned inside out. In essence like a stained shirt turned inside out; the stains are there but look faded. We have the same pain, but we are working on it. When you call yourself a survivor, you are still defining your life by that painful experience. If you want to define yourself as a survivor of a painful experience, and by that you mean you did not kill yourself because of it, I guess you are a survivor. But if your emotional and spiritual life is still frozen in time because of a painful event, you still nurse it, curse and rehearse it, you may be *surviving* but you are not healing and growing.

Look at this life-changing verse:

> **But thanks be to God! He gives us the victory through our Lord Jesus Christ.**
> 1 Corinthians 15:57

Please notice what the verse does not say. It does not say that you *survive* because of Jesus Christ. The verse clearly states that you have victory because of Jesus Christ. This is what I want, and I am sure this is what you want, a life of victory; a life that is not defined by, or limited by, the pain we experience here on this earth, but rather a life that rises above chaos. A life that overcomes the periods of emotional death we experience, and rises again to a new life and

Aisle Five | Renovate and Redecorate

purpose. This is not the life of a survivor, rather the life of a victor.

When Paul wrote these verses in Corinthians, it was in response to the crucifixion and resurrection of Jesus Christ. When Christ was crucified, he took sin with him to the cross. Sin was nailed with Christ on the cross. That means he experienced all the pain that sin delivered. He bore it. The power of sin died right along with him. He rose again on the third day proving the power of sin had no affect on him.

Christ turns to you and offers you that same resurrection power over sin in your life, so that you do not have to remain a victim or even be a survivor, but you can become a victor; never again allowing your life to be defined by sin or by *any sin perpetrated on you by others*.

> **Or don't you know that all of us who were baptized into Christ Jesus were baptized into his death? We were therefore buried with him through baptism into death in order that, just as Christ was raised from the dead through the glory of the Father, we too may live a new life.**
> Romans 6:3-4

If you have committed your life to Christ, and declared that commitment by baptism, Christ's death becomes your death and Christ's life becomes your life. You too may live a new life, not just in some future state, but right now. A new life is not an old life turned inside out; not the life of a victim or even a survivor. A new life of victory is what Jesus offers you.

The Relationship Depot

Check out how the Apostle John expresses this:

> **This is love for God: to obey his commands. And his commands are not burdensome, for everyone born of God overcomes the world. This is the victory that has overcome the world, even our faith. Who is it that overcomes the world? Only he who believes that Jesus is the Son of God.**
> 1 John 5:3-5

Notice he writes, in the second line, that every one born of God overcomes the world. When you and I declare that we are Christ's and that he is ours, we have been born to a new life in Christ, one that is designed to overcome the world. This new life, given to us by Christ, has the power to overcome the affects of the world's system on us. It's a sinful system with one objective: to destroy you emotionally, spiritually and physically.

Faith in Jesus Christ and what he secured for you by his death and resurrection is the basis for you living a victorious life. That faith is activated, or demonstrated as being real, by your obedience to his commands.

Imagine you have someone imprisoned in the jail of your heart. You have an event you are holding onto that defines your life, either as a victim or a survivor. The Bible says that as a believer in Jesus Christ, you are a victor. How do you get there? You must obey Gods commands. (1 John 5:3)

You have nursed it, cursed it, and rehearsed it; the Bible says you must…

REVERSE IT

Aisle Five | Renovate and Redecorate

Read this verse out loud:

> Ye have heard that it hath been said, Thou shalt love thy neighbour, and hate thine enemy. But I say unto you, Love your enemies, bless them that curse you, do good to them that hate you, and pray for them which despitefully use you, and persecute you; That ye may be the children of your Father which is in heaven.
> Matthew 5:43-45 (KJV)

Victory and freedom from the residual effects of hurt and abuse that can destroy the very core of your being is available to you when you choose the opposite of what the world's values tell you. Stick with me here, even though your brain may be setting up its shields and defences. At least hear me out. In the verse above, Jesus himself states that to break the affect of an emotional or spiritual stranglehold that someone, or some event, has on your life, you need to move forward using love; not hate, not revenge, but love. Jesus is even so bold as to say that you are to, "Love your enemies, bless them that curse you, do good to them that hate you, and pray for them which despitefully use you, and persecute you."

When Jesus tells you to love your enemy, he is not asking you to love the person who hurt you with the earthly love of affection. Jesus defines the actions of an enemy as one who curses you, shows hatred, does things out of spite to you and persecutes you. Joan's father needed to be stopped from hurting his little child. Jesus is saying that the person who caused you such great pain is in need of his love. He wants you to let Jesus himself love them through you. Jesus is well aware that you are not able to love your enemy in your own strength and power. He understands that this is an impossible

The Relationship Depot

request for you. But it is not an impossible request for him, if you will let him.

Jesus loves through you by asking you to bless them that curse you. Stop the nursing, cursing and rehearsing. Stop using derogatory words towards those who hurt you and stop swearing and cursing this person out. It is entirely within the realm of your power to no longer tear this person down, in your mind, or to other people. Ask God to give you the desire, and then, the power to do this. He has promised that to you. Be silent. The cursing may express your pain, but it does not help you heal. Be careful to avoid making it a habit and allowing it to take a strong hold over you. Once the habit takes hold, it will be able to plant seeds of bitterness and thereafter, emotional cancer can take root.

Try this for a second, an hour or a day. Every time the negative thoughts race through your mind, capture them, and tell them you have now turned that person over to Jesus. They are his issue to deal with as he sees fit. Every day, you will get stronger in this area of your life as you constantly turn this person over to Jesus.

God promises:

> **Do not take revenge, my friends, but leave room for God's wrath, for it is written: "It is mine to avenge; I will repay," says the Lord. On the contrary: "If your enemy is hungry, feed him; if he is thirsty, give him something to drink. In doing this, you will heap burning coals on his head." Do not be overcome by evil, but overcome evil with good.**
> Romans 12:19-21

Aisle Five | Renovate and Redecorate

God expressly commands you to not seek revenge. The reason you are not to seek revenge is because God is better at bringing justice, and punishing than you ever will be. God is the judge. God is the great equalizer. God will bring justice. God will punish those who perpetrate pain on other human beings. God will right all wrongs; you and I must trust him with that task. We must learn to defer to him and trust him.

It may be a challenge if you have been hurt and do not see justice. You may be asking yourself where God was the first time. If he was not my defender and protector then, how can I trust him to do what he says now? I want to remind you at this point, that there is so much more to life than the duration of our earthly existence. Life can seem so unfair, unjust, and full of pain. God has promised that a day will come when every tear will be wiped away. (Revelation 21:4) Until we experience that day, we must continue to trust in a Just and Holy God who will make all things right, including dealing justly and fairly with those who create earthly pain through abuse, abandonment, neglect, broken promises, violence and the like.

Jesus says we must let this vengeful spirit go. This is not a Spirit of God but a spirit of the world's system. The first thing we can do is stop and reverse the flow of bitterness out from our lives by simply refusing to curse any more. The basic act of ceasing to curse the situation is the catalyst that releases God's love to flow into the situation. Where God's love flows there is healing. There is one more step. Are you still with me? The next step in becoming a victor is to…

DISPERSE IT

This is the stage where you get rid of all the emotional baggage you have been carrying. You give it away, you break it up, you have an emotional yard sale, and you clean your spiritual house. Just like the dispersants used to break up the oil spilled in the Gulf Coast into tiny, individual particles, so the love of God will give you the power to break up the strongholds in your emotional life into tiny pieces for disposal.

Let's return to Jesus' statements in Matthew.

> **Love your enemies, bless them that curse you, do good to them that hate you, and pray for them which despitefully use you, and persecute you;**
> Matthew 5:44(KJV)

You are now at the action stage of experiencing victory. Jesus says you are to "do good" to those that hate you. The mental process of being quiet and allowing God to be God in this situation is now moving you forward to a place where your words must become deeds. Perhaps you cannot ever see yourself doing something good for the person you have held a grudge against for so long. But I am certain that as you take the beginning step of quietening your vengeful thoughts, you will begin to experience the new power of self-control emerging within you.

Think of the freedom you will have with this person not controlling your thoughts any longer. Think of the emotional and spiritual peace that will come with this. Think of what it will mean to you to be able to pray for that person, to do something good for that person. This

Aisle Five | Renovate and Redecorate

may be a frightening thought, and that is understandable.

At the end of Romans 12:19-21, Paul quotes Jesus as saying, **"If your enemy is hungry, feed him; if he is thirsty, give him something to drink. In doing this, you will heap burning coals on his head."** Paul adds his own commentary to Jesus' words when he writes the line, **"Do not be overcome by evil, but overcome evil with good."**

This last line is the principle you want to be striving for. You are not to be overcome by evil, or by thoughts of revenge that keep you awake, or by hours of nursing, rehearsing and cursing your situation. Instead, you must be prepared to do good when the opportunity presents itself. I do not believe that you are being asked to run out right now and do something good to someone who has hurt you. Jesus, in Matthew 5, states that when you repay good for evil, then you are a true child, a true likeness of your father which is in heaven.

What Jesus is asking you to do is to grow emotionally and spiritually to the point, that if the opportunity presents itself to do good, you would be prepared to do so. The very act of doing something good, when presented with an opportunity to do so, destroys the powerful strongholds of evil that you have built up in your life. You may have the opportunity to say hello, when you would rather turn away. You may have the opportunity to forward a piece of mail, when you would rather throw it in the trash. An opportunity to do good actually can be simple. It has been my experience that the Lord will never place you in a situation of doing good for which he has not already prepared your heart. However, he may push you a bit and help you to grow.

You may have the opportunity for reconciliation, which is possible only when the person who harmed you has repented. That means they have turned their behavior around, changed behavior and no longer act in a hurtful way towards you. Reconciliation allows for intimacy to be restored or achieved. If they choose not to change their behavior, you can forgive, just without reconciliation. When there is no repentance, you may need to step out of the way and let God do his work.

Everything rises and falls on forgiveness.

When the disciples asked Jesus how they should pray he responded in this manner and said,

> Pray, then, in this way: 'Our Father who is in heaven, Hallowed be Your name. Your kingdom come Your will be done, On earth as it is in heaven. Give us this day our daily bread. And forgive us our debts, as we also have forgiven our debtors. 'And do not lead us into temptation, but deliver us from evil. [For Yours is the kingdom and the power and the glory forever. Amen.]'
> Matthew 6:9-13 (NASB)

Please note the line that reads, **"forgive us our debts, as we also have forgiven our debtors."** The words, **"as we also have forgiven"**, is an important message regarding forgiveness. God's forgiveness is tied directly to your forgiveness. The prayer states that God will forgive you to the same degree that you have forgiven others.

Here are two often overlooked verses at the end of this prayer:
> **For if you forgive others for their transgressions, your heavenly Father will also forgive you. But if you do not**

forgive others, then your Father will not forgive your transgressions.
Matthew 6:14-15 (NASB)

These are conditional statements. If you do something, God will do something. If you do not do something, God will not do something. They are very blunt statements, spoken by Jesus, so that there could be no mistake, or misinterpretation. You experience the forgiveness of God in your life in direct proportion to which you forgive. God has chosen to tie his forgiveness of us to our forgiveness of others.

I have spent hours trying to find at least one way around these verses that would give me the right to nurse a grudge, hold a resentment, nurture some bitterness, plot revenge, justify my anger, excuse my temper, or rationalize my disobedience, but I cannot find a way. Lack of forgiveness on my part, for any reason, blocks the flow of God's grace into my life. My unforgiving spirit becomes an impenetrable barrier to the nurturing, healing and forgiving work of the Holy Spirit in me.

The reason so many Christians find their spiritual life as dry as the Sahara desert is because they have developed a stronghold of not forgiving in their lives that chokes the life of the Spirit of God. They read the Bible, but they are bored. They attend worship service, but find the service dull. Spiritual issues are slowly losing their attraction, but they cannot admit it. They are running on spiritual fumes; the tank is empty and not being replenished. Nothing seems to work; not another Bible study, nor another revival meeting, nor another burst of charismatic activity. The feelings of peace they had when they started their walk with the Lord are gone. All spiritual roads seem to be leading to an empty disconnectedness, devoid of vibrancy and meaning. Is it true of someone you know, a friend, a spouse, a child? Is this true of you?

Read carefully my words. God has not changed. He is the same yesterday, today and forever. (Hebrews 13:8) God is also abiding by his word and his laws; these have not changed either. Most of the people I meet whose spiritual life has dried up are carrying very heavy backpacks full of resentment. They are still nursing, cursing and rehearsing, with ever increasing intensity. It is time to undo the straps of the backpack, slip out from the grip of the harness and let the weight of unforgiveness crash to the floor. It is time to be free.

Forgiveness brings freshness.

Whenever I mess up and need to get back on track, I open the book of Psalms. David was a professional shepherd with amazing musical ability. The Psalms are a collection of his songs. There is a reality to David's writing because he experienced life full on. He was a star teenager who killed a giant, went on to be a king, commit adultery, put a contract killing out on his lover's husband, experienced the death of his child, and was renewed and restored by God. Here is one of my favourite Psalms:

> Praise the LORD, O my soul; all my inmost being, praise his holy name.
>
> Praise the LORD, O my soul, and forget not all his benefits who forgives all your sins and heals all your diseases, who redeems your life from the pit and crowns you with love and compassion, who satisfies your desires

Aisle Five | Renovate and Redecorate

with good things so that your youth is renewed like the eagle's.
Psalm 103:1-5

David begins to praise God from the very core of his being in verse 1. He reminds himself that the benefit of knowing God is that he forgives and heals in verses 2 and 3. He also declares that God redeems, or buys back, those who have fallen into the most horrible of places, the cesspools of life in verse 4. God cleans off your filth and restores you so completely, it is as if you are crowned, clothed and covered head to toe with his compassion. God also takes the desires that so often lead you into the pit and replaces them with healthy desires, which lighten your spirit and release your mind so that in the end you feel like a kid who can fly in verse 5.

This is God's offer to you today - forgiveness, healing, redemption, compassion, and a renewed life. The question, is do you want to be well?

Here are the lyrics to one of my favourite songs by Phil McHugh to start you on your journey so that you can fly once again above the pain, sorrow, bitterness and resentment.

> A fervent prayer rose up to heaven,
> A fragile soul was losing ground
> Sorting through this earthly babble,
> Heaven heard the sound.
> It was a life of no distinction,
> No successes, only tries.
> Yet, gazing down on this unlovely one,
> There was love in Heaven's Eyes.

The orphaned child, the wayward father,
The homeless traveler in the rain
When life goes by and no one bothers,
Heaven feels the pain.
Looking down, God sees each heartache,
Knows each sorrow, hears each cry,
And looking up, we'll see compassion's
Fire ablaze in Heaven's Eyes .

Refrain:
In Heaven's Eyes, there are no losers,
In Heaven's Eyes, no hopeless cause.
Only people like you, with feelings like me
And we're amazed at the grace we can find
In Heaven's Eyes.

God is waiting for you. Here is a little prayer that will open the flood gates to God's healing and restoration in your life right now. Pray out loud if possible.

Dear Jesus,

Forgive me for carrying this unforgiveness for so long. With your help and by your power, I now release this situation (name it) to you. I give it to you and I ask that your Spirit renew and restore me. I no longer want to live as a victim or a survivor. I want to live in the victory that you secured for me by your death and resurrection. Thank you for forgiving me as I release my unforgiveness to you. Thank you for helping me to fly again.

This I ask in Jesus' name. Amen.

Review

Talking about fear in the last chapter, this emotion can get lodged in our hearts and thwart us from making changes that God is asking from us. Growing into the men and women God calls us to be requires change and the courage to follow Jesus Christ's lead.

We may be crying about our pain but too fearful to trust God with the change to come. Like the man at the pool, he could have been healed 38 years earlier yet he chose self-pity instead. Fear will steal our faith and trust in Christ to heal our pain; a pain that comes with you into your relationships and damages intimacy. Resentment and unforgiveness take root, just like the old man's resistance to getting help.

Everything rises and falls on forgiveness.

Biblical Instructions

Now there is in Jerusalem near the Sheep Gate a pool, which in Aramaic is called Bethesda and which is surrounded by five covered colonnades. Here a great number of disabled people used to lie—the blind, the lame, the paralyzed. One who was there had been an invalid for thirty-eight years. When Jesus saw him lying there and learned that he had been in this condition for a long time, he asked him, "Do you want to get well?"

"Sir," the invalid replied, "I have no one to help me into the pool when the water is stirred. While I am trying to get in, someone else goes down ahead of me."

Then Jesus said to him, "Get up! Pick up your mat and walk." At once the man was cured; he picked up his mat and walked.

The day on which this took place was a Sabbath.

John 5:2-9

But thanks be to God! He gives us the victory through our Lord Jesus Christ.

I Corinthians 15:57

In fact, this is love for God: to keep his commands. And his commands are not burdensome, for everyone born of God overcomes the world. This is the victory that has overcome the world, even our faith. Who is it that overcomes the world? Only the one who believes that Jesus is the Son of God.

I John 5:3-5

"You have heard that it was said, 'Love your neighbor and hate your enemy.' But I tell you, love your enemies and pray for those who persecute you, that you may be children of your Father in heaven. He causes his sun to rise on the evil and the good, and sends rain on the righteous and the unrighteous.

Matthew 5:43-45

Do not take revenge, my dear friends, but leave room for God's wrath, for it is written: "It is mine to avenge; I will repay," says the Lord.

On the contrary:

If your enemy is hungry, feed him;
if he is thirsty, give him something to drink.
In doing this, you will heap burning coals on his head.
Do not be overcome by evil, but overcome evil with good.

Romans 12:19-21

This, then, is how you should pray:
Our Father in heaven,
hallowed be your name,
your kingdom come,
your will be done,
on earth as it is in heaven.
Give us today our daily bread.
And forgive us our debts,
as we also have forgiven our debtors.
And lead us not into temptation,
but deliver us from the evil one.'

Matthew 6:9-13

The Relationship Depot

Building activities

1. Is there an area in your life that Jesus is asking you the question, "Do you want to get well?"

2. List people you are having trouble setting free through forgiveness?

3. What do you think is getting in the way of your forgiveness?

4. How is not forgiving a benefit to you?

5. Begin to pray for the people you listed in #2. Start by asking God to be kind to them.

Aisle Six
The Smart Home, Wired for Good Communication

You need to find a way to say precisely what you mean. This is good advice from the trusted governess, Mary Poppins. This advice goes a long way in the marriage relationship where miscommunication is the enemy in many arguments.

Here is an example taken from my own life of communication gone awry. Eileen and I were on our way home from a party. The air in the car was blue with anger and innuendo. Perhaps you have been in a similar situation. This fight was all about miscommunication. Sound familiar? Here is the conversation, at the party, that led to the car scene.

"Do you want to go?" asks Eileen.

"Let's stay for a while, is that Ok?" asks Jeremy
"Well, I guess so," she replies with resignation.

So we stayed, and when we arrived home the conversation was resumed.

Aisle Six | The Smart Home, Wired for Good Communication

"I really didn't want to stay, you know," says Eileen to Jeremy with some anger in her voice.

"You didn't?" Jeremy asks.

"You should have known that," she retorts.

"How was I supposed to know you didn't want to stay? You asked me my opinion, I gave it to you and you said 'I guess so'," Jeremy defends.

"Well, I really didn't mean that," his wife replies.

"How was I supposed to know that?" he explains.

"You just should have," she barks back and leaves the room.

This incident, early in our relationship, helped us to establish a principle of communication that we still use to this day; ask what you really want, and say what you really mean. The next time, Eileen very clearly told me she wanted to go home, and while I said I wanted to stay, I was willing to leave. Ask what you want, and say what you mean. There is no need for guessing or making assumptions. This takes some practice, especially if sharing your needs has been challenged by others in the past.

While communication is both non-verbal and verbal, words have a unique power to them. When you read the account of creation in Genesis, you will discover that God created the world using words. In those opening chapters, time and time again we read how God said, "Let there be…" Let there be oceans; let there be birds; let there be sky; let there be stars; and in every instance, what God asked for materialized.

In the New Testament (Matthew 21:19), Jesus got a little ticked at a fig tree that was not bearing fruit at the proper time. He cursed the fig tree; he said "die" and the fig tree died.

Words, when they are spoken, never disappear.

> But I tell you that everyone will have to give account on the Day of Judgment for every empty word they have spoken.
> Matthew 12:36

There is a power inherent in words that requires us to take what we say and how we say it very seriously. There are some scientists who believe that every sound wave ever emitted is still going through the universe. It is simply going further away. We cannot hear it any longer because its amplitude has died out, but that sound continues into the very reaches of the universe. Jesus tells us that you will have to give an account. God will ask why you used careless words, the hurtful words and used his name in vain. What could the reason be for using careless words?

> For by your words you will be acquitted and by your words you will be condemned.
> Matthew 12:37

God will not condemn or acquit you. God will not stand in judgement over you; however, he will use your own words as the basis for his judgement.

Words are important to your salvation.

That if you declare with your mouth, "Jesus is Lord," and believe in your heart that God raised him from the dead, you will be saved. For it is with your heart that you believe and are justified, and it is with your mouth that you profess your faith and are saved.
Romans 10:9-10

For salvation by faith to become active in your life it requires a verbal declaration. Words set in motion your salvation. You believe in your heart and speak that belief using words. The bible says **"it is with your mouth that you confess and are saved"**.

Take a look at James 3:6 (MSG). James has some strong comments to make about the tongue: **"The tongue also is a fire"**. Have you ever been the victim of somebody's fiery tongue? Or maybe you have been the perpetrator of a fiery tongue? Have you ever had someone unleash the fury of their tongue on you and burn you to your very spirit by their cruel words? **"...a world of evil among the parts of the body. It corrupts the whole person, sets the whole course of his life on fire."**

Have you ever said something that got you into trouble or took your life for a detour? You said something like, "Well, maybe we should just get a divorce." You did not really mean those careless words; you were just making a power play. Someone called you on it and then, there goes your life.

James goes on to say (the tongue) **"is itself set on fire by hell"**. Wow, that is a direct connection between hell and my mouth. Have you ever considered that the enemy of your spirit, the one who

The Relationship Depot

desires relationships, marriages and families to be destroyed, has direct access to your mouth? When you speak forth words that hurt, pierce, divide, wound, and destroy, you are the mouth piece of hell itself. I do not want my mouth, tongue and consequently, my words, to be the spokesperson for hell and all its destruction. I do not think you want that either.

> **All kinds of animals, birds, reptiles and creatures of the sea are being tamed and have been tamed by mankind, but no human being can tame the tongue. It is a restless evil, full of deadly poison.**
> James 3:7-8

He then explains how deceitful the tongue can be.

> **With the tongue we praise our Lord and Father, and with it we curse human beings, who have been made in God's likeness. Out of the same mouth come praise and cursing. My brothers and sisters, this should not be.**
> James 3:9-10

Years ago the worst time for my unruly tongue would have to be when my family and I were trying to get out the door for church on Sunday morning.

"Ok, 5 minutes to be in the car!" I hollered.

I was ready but no one else was ready to join me. The kids had the wrong shoes. Eileen had the wrong purse. Five minutes turned into 10 and all of a sudden my angry words flowed like a broken fire hydrant. The commander of the automobile unleashed his wrath, the kids cried and Eileen got very silent. I probably made some very cryptic comments on the ride between my driveway and the front of the church. I walked into church after saying some very cruel things to my family. I got up in front of the congregation and shouted "Halleluiah, praise God, let's rejoice together in his goodness today." I was a walking poster board for James' comments:

> **Out of the same mouth come praise and cursing. My brothers and sisters, this should not be.**
> James 3:10

Thanks to God and the taming of my tongue, I am doing better today. But I am always stunned at how easily I can fall back into my old habits.

We can find wisdom about the spoken word in the Old Testament. In the book of Proverbs there are nuggets of wisdom for life and health. With 31 chapters, there is one for every day of the month.

> **Like apples of gold in settings of silver is a ruling rightly given. Like an earring of gold or an ornament of fine gold is the rebuke of a wise judge to a listening ear.**
> Proverbs 25:11-12

When someone wise comes along, giving you insight and coaching about yourself, those are wise words for you to capture. There is perhaps no greater uplifting experience than to hear wise words, spoken by a wise person, and addressed directly to your situation. I want to grow into being that wise person, with good words. Perhaps you do too.

> **The words of the reckless pierce like swords, but the tongue of the wise brings healing.**
> Proverbs 12:18

The Relationship Depot

Have you ever been pierced by someone's words? I would take a broken arm any day over a broken heart. I would rather take some part of my body, broken or bruised, than to have someone say cruel, mean or ugly things to me; or comments that are able to get through my armour and inside me, penetrating the very core of my being. Do you know I still remember words that were said to me as a teenager growing up? I bet you do too. I am now over 60 years old and I still remember those words. I also recall the incidents where people used cruel words towards me. Even though God has healed the emotional response to those words, they are still in my memory bank. I can still hear them. I also know that there are people who can still recall the hurtful words I said to them. My prayer is that they can forgive me and allow God's grace to heal their spirits. There are people who remember your words as well. Perhaps a prayer of forgiveness for those hurtful words would be in order.

The last half of Proverbs 12:18 states:

> **But the tongue of the wise brings healing.**

Has anyone ever said words that were perfect for you in that moment? Do you ever open the Word of God and let his words speak to you in your spirit and suddenly find a moment of healing and renewal?

> **A gentle answer turns away wrath, but a harsh word stirs up anger.**
> Proverbs 15:1

Have you ever escalated an argument? You know the words are getting hurtful and more out of control. You know exactly what button to push in that other person. After 36 years, I know my wife's hot buttons by heart. Sometimes I just want to push her a bit over

Aisle Six | The Smart Home, Wired for Good Communication

the edge. I know exactly what to say in the situation to make her blow. You probably know the same responses in your spouse. But God wants you to answer gently and not escalate the situation. Sometimes you need to keep quiet. Stop fuelling the fire. Stop pushing emotional buttons. Take a break. Go for a walk. Flatly refuse to escalate an argument. Make a deal with your spouse that you will honour God when you argue, and stop hurting each other with unnecessary words.

I remember a more recent argument in our relationship that got away from me. I knew I was right. I was sure I was right. I still am sure that I was right. For some reason we were unable to recover from this spat. This was one of the very, very few times in our marriage that we could not resolve the issue before bedtime. The next day Eileen was up and out to her office, and things were not going well. I wondered what radical, unexpected thing I could do to deflate this disagreement. It was then that God's wisdom prevailed. I called the florist and had them send a bouquet of yellow roses (our special flower) to her office. My gesture of letting go of this particular battle created harmony between us again. It was not important who was right or wrong.

I have used many cruel and manipulative words. Both my wife and I have a marvellous command of the English language. If you ever want to experience a good sabre fight you should drop into our house when we have an argument. At some point, we have to say "stop this" before we really hurt each other. We made a commitment to stop wounding each other with our words. That commitment is to each other and to God. I strongly recommend you do the same.

> **The tongue has the power of life and death, and those who love it will eat its fruit.**
> Proverbs 18:21

The power of the tongue has life and death in it. In the spirit realm you have the power to speak a word of faith into someone's life, a word of healing, hope, encouragement and forgiveness. You can build someone up, raise their spirits and bring joy with your words. You also have the power to speak death into someone with cruel and hurtful words, to deflate their spirit, disempower their dreams, and corrode their sense of self.

I would rather be a person who speaks words of life every day, not words of death. Imagine being in a relationship with someone whose very words bring life and excitement to your spirit. Imagine the excitement waking up each day to that person's voice knowing that you are growing in a verbally safe environment. Imagine the peace, security and sense of freedom, living in that environment could bring. God gives you the power, through your words, to create that type of environment for your spouse, children, friends, co-workers, and church members. Life or death is only a word away.

Returning to James, we read some of the most appropriate words regarding communication written in the Bible:

> **My dear brothers and sisters, take note of this: Everyone should be quick to listen, slow to speak and slow to become angry, for man's anger does not bring about the righteous life that God desires.**
> James 1:19-20

Listen more, speak less, and remove the anger from your

communication. I admit this is a tough one for me, but I want to please the Lord. So if that means shutting up, actively listening and finding ways to communicate without anger, I am all for it. How about you?

Here is a joke that brings this point home. A guy came to his pastor and said, "Reverend, I only have one talent."

The pastor asked, "What's your talent?"

The man said, "I have the gift of criticism." The pastor was wise and replied, "The Bible says that the guy who had only one talent went out and buried it. Maybe that's what you ought to do with yours." Get it?

To help you communicate and relate better in your marriage and other relationships, consider applying my Top 10 Principles of Communication.

My Top 10 Principles of Communication

10. THE ISSUE IS NEVER THE ISSUE. POWER IS **AL**WAYS THE ISSUE. Any argument you have ever had with your spouse, your children, or co-workers, no matter the topic, the issue at hand is not what you are really fighting about. It is not the fact that you squeezed the toothpaste from the wrong end, not the fact that you put the toilet paper roll on backwards, or that you overspent your budget. The real issue is always power. The issue is always who has the control at the moment. Will it be my way or your way?

This same principle applies to issues that arise in an office setting when people try to communicate and resolve issues. No one wants to give up their little bit of power. When you come together in a relationship, something inside of you wants to know who has the power? You see it when people break agreements in relationships by flirting, buying sports equipment without a spouse's agreement, or hanging out with friends not favoured by a spouse. When the issue is an affair, the stakes are higher and more challenging to repair.

The broken agreement shifts the power. The offender gets caught and the 'catcher' gets to decide punishment. The real challenge becomes putting the relationship back together with the balance of power restored. Maybe, as the relationship starts to come back together, the 'catcher' likely enjoys some of the extra power they experienced. Or the 'catcher' starts to cooperate and rebuild trust by giving back some of the extra power. But if the 'catcher' will not release that power, and become whole with their partner by restoring the balance of power, then the relationship never recovers.

Guarding power in your relationship will only ensure your arguments will never come to an end, because power is always the issue. Perhaps the next time you get into some kind of disagreement or argument with your spouse, you should stop and ask yourself, what is really going on? Is this really about the issue or am I pushing this to the wall, demanding my own way and marching forward because I need power and I need to be in control?

9. UNDERSTAND THE DIFFERENCE BETWEEN INFLUENCE & CONTROL

When you are sharing an idea or suggestion with your family, are you seeking to provide insight that may influence the outcome of a family decision, or are you seeking control?

There is a really big distinction between influence and control. When I am talking with my wife, I want to help influence the decision we are seeking together. The influence approach considers both of our viewpoints so that they can be taken into account in the final decision. This is a very different communication style than deciding that you will be in control. On the other hand, the control approach results in you taking a stand that your choices are foremost. That approach sounds very much like "I am going to paint the house the colour I want and I don't care what my wife thinks. I will talk her into doing things my way". Rather than seeking to influence, one person takes control. Influence requires different actions than control. You must learn to listen more and speak less. Avoid anger, because anger in a discussion can be a sign of moving to control tactics.

In your relationship, it is vital to be aware of the difference in needing to control or wanting to influence. Are you trying to control your children's lives? Truthfully, most children feel that way. I would rather influence their lives. I want to share my beliefs and my values. I want to lay it out for them, but what I ultimately want is to help influence their path. Their final decision may not be exactly what I want. But if I have an opportunity to give input into that decision then I have fulfilled my role as parental influencer, not controller.

8. THE PURPOSE OF COMMUNICATION IS TO UNDERSTAND THE OTHER PERSON'S PERSPECTIVE

Here is a prayer by St Francis of Assisi which can be used as a model for our communications with each other.

> Lord, make me an instrument of your peace,
> Where there is hatred, let me sow love;
> where there is injury, pardon;
> where there is doubt, faith;
> where there is despair, hope;
> where there is darkness, light;
> where there is sadness, joy;
>
> O Divine Master, grant that I may not so much seek to be consoled as to console;
> **to be understood as to understand**;
> to be loved as to love.
>
> For it is in giving that we receive;
> it is in pardoning that we are pardoned;
> and it is in dying that we are born to eternal life.

Consider the line bolded in the above verse, **to be understood as to understand**. Understanding the meaning of these words is a key to effective communication. He is elegantly saying that it is not as important for me to make you understand me as it is for me to understand you.

"Now wait a minute," I can hear you say. You want your point of view to be understood, and you need your partner to understand what you are saying. I agree with you. I am just suggesting that the best way for you to be understood, is to let the other person go first. Be

Aisle Six | The Smart Home, Wired for Good Communication

sure you let them know that you understand their point of view, then ask if you can share yours. People listen much more carefully to what someone has to say when they feel they have been heard first. People who have had adequate time to express their point of view also interrupt less. They feel safe; they have been heard.

Try it with your kids. Listen to them all the way through without interruption or argument. Now you have earned the right to be heard. They should be taught to return the same courtesy of listening to you all the way through, without interruption.

How many times have you been talking about an issue when somebody says to you, "Are we talking about the same thing?" Since neither person was listening to the other, it took forever to come to the realization that you were both on the same side, just using different words. If you take that concept and try to figure out how to make it happen in your life, what would change in the way you communicate? When Eileen and I have a decision to make together, no matter the issue, my primary purpose is to thoroughly and completely come to grips with her point of view. That means I am not cutting her off when I think I know what she is going to say. I listen and then I use three powerful words: "help me understand".

Help me understand why you want to paint the walls deep sea green. Help me understand why you get so nervous when I blow the limit on the credit card. Help me understand why "this issue" triggers you. Help me come to grips with what troubles you and let me get inside your brain and come to understand what brings you to this moment.

Most of us do not ask such questions. More likely we ask accusing questions. "Why did you spend so much on the credit card?"

Insults often get in there too like, "What's the matter with you? Don't you know we don't have enough money?"

I encourage you to abandon all accusing questions; they just create defensiveness in the other person. Practice using the phrase "help me understand" at work, at home and in church. You will be amazed at how calm and focused your communication with others will become. You will also learn about others and others will listen to you. The very thing you wanted from the beginning.

7. DEATH TO SELF, OTHERS FIRST

Our walk with Jesus Christ is a path that says less of me and more of him. It is a way that models death to what I want and life to what he wants. This approach constantly takes me out of the front seat, and into the second seat and, if necessary, into the backseat. That is the journey of Christianity.

The journey of relationships is similar to declaring death to self, less of you and more of the other person. Consider then how you need to communicate. Death to what you want to say and life to hearing what your spouse needs to say. This simple shift alone is spiritually profound, and can be difficult to act on. But this shift of understanding that you are in a relationship with the emphasis on the other person can be life-enhancing.

Why is it about the other person? The marriage relationship is really about God and it cannot be about God if you have to have your own way all the time. The more you seek to understand the other person, the more they want to listen to you. The outcome is reciprocal.

Aisle Six | The Smart Home, Wired for Good Communication

The whole principle of Christianity is that in giving we are given, in pardoning we are pardoned, and in losing ourselves we find ourselves.

Here is how this concept is revealed in the Bible.

> **Love from the center of who you are; don't fake it. Run for dear life from evil; hold on for dear life to good. Be good friends who love deeply; practice playing second fiddle.**
> Romans 12:9-10 (MSG)

Have you heard of the second fiddle? In an orchestra, there are several rows of violins. The first row, closest to the conductor, is most important. These violinists get all the exciting, difficult and demanding parts of the musical score. The second fiddles, seated in the next row, play parts that are really boring, maybe a little bit of harmony. They do not get the fancy notes that the first violins receive. However, without second violins, there would be no harmony, no one to fill in missing musical pieces. Second violins bring a richness and completeness to the musical sound. Their musical score may not be as demanding as the first violins, yet they are absolutely necessary for the music to sound beautiful.

What would happen if you chose to play second fiddle in your relationship? Say to yourself, I am going to sit in the second row of this relationship; not take the lead, follow a bit and see what happens. I am not going to always go first, talk first, drive first, line up at the buffet first, draw attention to my needs, or clamour for attention. Try it for a week and see what happens!

6. DISCOVER THE SOURCE OF ANGER USING A-H-E-N

No one can make you angry unless you chose to be angry - a truth that is sometimes hard to accept. There is a process for you becoming angry. Anger does not just pop out of nowhere.

Here is a little acronym that can help you in mastering anger in your communication.

A - When you see Anger

H - it is usually covering a Hurt. If you peek under that Hurt,

E – you will see you had an Expectation.

N - And if you look under that Expectation, you'll find a Need.

Take a moment now to recall a time when your anger surfaced in a discussion. See if you can put this little system to the test. It may take you several times to dig down and follow through each letter, but when you do, you will unmask the root source of your anger. Then you can ask God to help fill the need that is driving your behaviour. Do you remember that earlier we quoted from scripture that stated 'My God shall supply all your needs'? Do the work. God will provide. This may be another time for you to bring out the junk removal process that you developed earlier. Use the balloons, shredding paper, or burning scraps of lumber.

5. ASSUME POSITIVE INTENT

To assume positive intent means disciplining your mind to think the best, not the worst, of another person's intentions. Adopt a constant

Aisle Six | The Smart Home, Wired for Good Communication

attitude that the other person means well.

I remember a Friday afternoon in the summer waiting for Eileen outside the office building where she worked. I had packed up the car and got the twins all settled in, eager to head out to our cottage. Eileen called and asked to be picked up at 4:30. I was there right on time; after all, that is who I am, a right-on-time guy. I arrived at the front doors at 4:30. I looked at my watch; it was 4:35, and no Eileen. Other women met their rides, and I was still sitting there. By 4:50, I was steaming mad and muttering to myself.

"She's probably up there having another coffee and talking. Doesn't she know I am down here packed into a car with two fidgety kids and a growling stomach?"

The truth was that she had a work-related crisis. She was trying to solve a problem in order to help someone else. She was drafting an important briefing note for a government minister so he would have proper and reliable information to stand up in the Legislature. It took me a long time to turn around my 'stinking thinking', not assuming the worst all the time. Rather than focus on what inconvenienced me, I had to work hard to realize that Eileen no more wanted to work late on a summer Friday evening than I wanted to wait for her. It took me far too long to learn how to give my wife the benefit of the doubt, to choose calmness, and refuse to get angry. You can make the choice that your spouse intends well and that, under normal circumstances, they have your best interests at heart. They are not intentionally trying to upset you.

This goes for our children as well, especially when we are convinced that they are deliberately disobeying our rules. You start by being furious and think, "How dare he not obey my rules?"

Imagine your son does not get home by curfew, the time you both agreed on. Then the phone call comes and your son reports to you that his buddy, the one with the car, has been drinking, so your son chose not to ride home with him. In a second, your negative thinking about the curfew violation has been replaced with a sense of pride that your son displayed the common sense to call you for a ride home rather than ride with a drunk. Life would calm down considerably if we would just assume positive intent more often.

4. ACCEPT RESPONSIBILITY AND AIM FOR CLARITY

Here is a radical communication idea. You are responsible for what you meant to say, and for how the other person interprets what you say. You might have to think about that for a while. Jesus said we would be judged by our words, period.

When we accept responsibility for how someone interprets our words, we are accepting responsibility to ensure we have been clearly understood. Many of us hurl our words to another person's mind and run like heck. This is like a person pulling the pin on a hand grenade and throwing it into a crowd. The words explode, there is a mess of misunderstanding and no one accepts the responsibility for clarity. Both you and I know people who take great pride in always speaking the truth. Many of these people do not stick around long enough to see if that truth has been heard accurately, or in the correct context. Take the time to ask the other person what they heard you say. You can even explain, "I want to be sure you heard me correctly." Or, "what did you hear me say?" In a few short moments of dialogue, a misunderstanding can be avoided. Take the time and accept the responsibility for how someone interprets the words you speak.

3. ALWAYS CHOOSE YOUR WORDS CAREFULLY

> **Do not let any unwholesome talk come out of your mouths, but only what is helpful for building others up according to their needs, that it may benefit those who listen.**
> Ephesians 4:29

In this world, no one has the right to be verbally abusive to anyone else. I have seen people talk to a boss in a much kinder manner than they do to their spouse. I have also seen people treat wayward employees nicer than they treat their children.

No matter what you may say to me, I retain the right to respond in an appropriate, Christ-like manner. Always speak to bring healing. The next time you are about to yell and let go a string of superlatives, consider this verse.

> **Let your conversation be always full of grace, seasoned with salt, so that you may know how to answer everyone.**
> Colossians 4:6

There is one thing that no one circumstance or situation can rob you of, and that is your attitude. Let your communication reflect your Christ-like attitude. If you cannot say something nice, then do not say anything at all. This may require you to be silent and listen.

2. AVOID SLEEPING ON ANGER

> **In your anger do not sin. Do not let the sun go down while you are still angry.**
> Ephesians 4:26

There is nothing worse for a relationship than going to bed when angry. The Bible tells us that doing so opens a little door for the devil to get into our lives. Going to bed angry is like leaving the back door of your spirit open and allowing the enemy to begin to plant seeds of bitterness. Anger, when continually slept upon, nourishes the seeds of bitterness and those seeds grow deep roots. Most bitter people I meet have huge unresolved anger issues with roots so deep that they can only be dug out by the specific intervention of the Holy Spirit, as they seek forgiveness and restoration.

We have a right to be upset at times, but do not use the anger for revenge, that is a power move.

> **Go ahead and be angry. You do well to be angry - but don't use your anger as fuel for revenge.**
> Ephesians 4:26 (MSG)

When Paul is talking about anger here, he is talking about giving expression to those situations that create frustration in our lives; he's not talking about a raging and wounding anger that frightens and destroys. Above all, we are told to not stay angry. Do not go to bed angry. Do not give the Devil that kind of foothold in your life. Even if you have to stay up late, deal with the anger before you sleep. You may not get the issue fully resolved, but you can disperse the anger. Pray with each other, and ask God for his release of your anger before your head hits the pillow.

Aisle Six | The Smart Home, Wired for Good Communication

1. LISTEN LIKE YOU MEAN IT

> Be completely humble and gentle; be patient, bearing with one another in love. Make every effort to keep the
>
> unity of the Spirit through the bond of peace.
> Ephesians 4:2-3

Listening has the power to change everything. Have you had someone say to you in frustration, "Are you listening to me?" Or maybe you have said that to someone. Being heard is important to us.

> My dear brothers and sisters, take note of this: Everyone should be quick to listen, slow to speak and slow to become angry, for human anger does not bring about the righteous life that God desires.
> James 1:19-20

Listening with your full attention creates a clear communication line, whether with one person or many. When it is between spouses, parents and children, brothers and sisters or friends, the information gets delivered far more effectively when the listener is sending back the message of full attention.

Speaking to the men, sometimes we need to check with our wives. "Is this one of those times I just need to listen and not find a solution?" This kind of conversation can actually be a time to relax and enjoy learning about your wife.

It does mean you stop what you are doing, make eye contact, beam with acceptance and do not interrupt or give advice. Keep in mind

The Relationship Depot

that listening does not mean you agree, it simply allows the other person to speak and be heard.

It does not get any plainer than the statements written above. These words must become the basis for communication in your marriage, with your children, with co-workers and church members.

I have really good news for you; Jesus speaks to you with redemptive words, which means he speaks healing into your life and he does that as you read his Word.

Aisle Six | The Smart Home, Wired for Good Communication

Review

You need to find a way to say precisely what you mean. Ask for what you really want, say what you really mean. How we communicate is so vital to the nature of our relationship. Although spoken communication accounts for only 30% of our overall message, our words are important.

Arguments can take place from harsh words said but also from what doesn't get said. An easy flow of kind yet honest words back and forth allows for couples to share themselves. The emotional junk comes out in our words. As said in Proverbs, the tongue has immense power, so learning to use it wisely will bring peace, love and healing.

Biblical Instructions

> **But I tell you that everyone will have to give account on the day of judgment for every empty word they have spoken. For by your words you will be acquitted, and by your words you will be condemned.**
>
> Matthew 12:36-37

> **All kinds of animals, birds, reptiles and sea creatures are being tamed and have been tamed by mankind, but no human being can tame the tongue. It is a restless evil, full of deadly poison. With the tongue we praise our Lord and Father, and with it we curse human beings, who have been made in God's likeness. Out of the same mouth come praise and cursing. My brothers and sisters, this should not be.**
>
> James 3:7-10

The tongue has the power of life and death, and those who love it will eat its fruit.

Proverbs 18:21

The words of the reckless pierce like swords, but the tongue of the wise brings healing.

Proverbs 12:18

A gentle answer turns away wrath, but a harsh word stirs up anger.

Proverbs 15:1

My dear brothers and sisters, take note of this: everyone should be quick to listen, slow to speak and slow to become angry, because human anger does not produce the righteousness that God desires.

James 1:19-20

Building Activities

1. Practice listening to a family member for 10 minutes. No opinions, no advice. Give them your complete attention.

Rate your response between 1 and 10.

2. Which of the 10 principles do you need to work on? Write out several actions you could take to improve that skill, then pick three to act on.

Aisle Seven
Your Lifetime Guarantee

I was being introduced at a police function by the head of our local government. Frank was a no-nonsense politician who let you know where you stood with him. Honesty, loyalty and frankness were his calling card. Frank was a big, burly and blunt man. As I approached the podium, he was duly reading off my bio sheet and suddenly stopped, turned to me and said, "So what is your success rate?" I was as mystified by this statement as any of the 400 officers gathered in the room.

"I know you can marry them, but how many of them stick? What's your success rate?"

The officers laughed; it was an amusing observation. I smiled and laughed along with everyone, but the answer is, *not enough.* Far too many couples recite their vows and then proceed to break them. The divorce rate among those professing to have a relationship with Christ is rapidly rising. Some statisticians report that the divorce rate among regular church attendees is now marginally higher than that of the general population. Along with fast food and instant

Aisle Seven | Your Lifetime Guarantee

information, we also have disposable, throw-away everything. Is it any wonder that in this cultural environment relationships cannot survive?

I have officiated at hundreds of weddings in my role as a pastor and police chaplain. I encourage as many people as possible to use the traditional wedding vows, because they are good vows, memorable and easy to recite. In those wedding ceremonies people vowed to love, honour and cherish one another. They made a commitment when they said to each other, "for richer, for poor, for better, for worse, in sickness, and in health, in joy and in sorrow, to love and to cherish, and to be faithful to you alone as long as we both shall live". I review these vows with couples and there is no escape clause, none whatsoever. When they said their wedding vows, they were committing to one another in an incredible way.

To get a different perspective on commitment we can look to football fans. The Green Bay Packers football team has one of the longest waiting lists for season tickets in all of professional sports. There are over 78,000 people on the list; many more names than there are current seats at Lambeau Field. Right now, the average wait time for season tickets is approximately 35 years. If you add your name to the list today, the estimated wait time would be well over 100 years. It also requires a monetary down payment and you must pay every year to maintain your name on the list. For this reason, it is not unusual for fans to designate a recipient for their season tickets in their wills or to place newborn infants on the waiting list after receiving a birth certificate. I do not know if you have ever watched a game in Green Bay, Wisconsin, but it seems like it is always 45

The Relationship Depot

degrees below zero and fans sit there with a piece of styrofoam cheese on their head. That's commitment.

You become what you are committed to.

If you are a committed Green Bay Packer fan, you will sit with cheese on your head. If you are committed to retrofitting and building a beautiful cottage, you will save and put all your time into renovating. And if you are committed to being in a marriage relationship, then you will find yourself learning to cooperate and compromise.

Being a pastor in the same city for over 30 years, brings with it a certain responsibility that stretches beyond church members. So it was no surprise when a wealthy business owner asked for an appointment to see me. He did not attend our church, however, he wanted to get my advice on his failing marriage. After opening pleasantries he informed me that he had decided to leave his wife of 25 years. According to him, he did not have a younger model waiting in the wings, he was just bored. His wife was dull, the kids were gone and it was time for a change.

To try and understand his situation better I asked a few pertinent questions. Had his wife been unfaithful? Not to his knowledge. Had she been sick or physically unresponsive? I was searching for the real reason this man wanted to walk away from the companion of his life, the mother of his children and the person who had worked with him diligently in the early years to build his business into the powerhouse that it had become. I could not find a reason, any reason, that made any sense to me, except he was bored. The spark was gone, the mystery unshrouded; she was yesterday's woman. It

Aisle Seven | Your Lifetime Guarantee

seemed like he wanted a change, like an oil change, a fresh coat of paint, a new rug, or an updated 3D television.

I asked him, "Do you know how much it is going to cost you to pay off the old model?"

He did not, but said he would get back to me, because that was a good question. Sure enough, he checked with his lawyer and accountant and returned to inform me that the residual buy out of his lease on the old Mrs. would be in the neighbourhood of 2.8 million dollars. I could not believe my ears; $2.8 million to dispose of his wife simply because he was bored? How bad can the old model be? Did he not think it was worth the effort to re-build their current relationship, keep the family intact, keep finances strong, even though it may be hard work? He went ahead and paid 2.8 million to leave his marriage. I saw him many months later and he did not appear to be happy at all; he was still searching for that perfect replacement model.

Time and again people sit in my office and complain that the spark is gone from their relationship. Something does not feel right they tell me, and they base their decisions on how they feel. All of a sudden, the relationship does not feel right and so they want out of it. Some people want the ER model and I am not talking about the television show. Sometimes they want the new*er* model, sometimes they want a *prettier* model, a *funnier* model, a *richer* model, a *sexier* model. They want the ER model. In our age of castaway this and castaway that, disposable, instant and fast, we go through relationship after relationship because we have not really come to understand commitment. For better, for worse, in sickness and in health, to love and to cherish or until something better strikes one's fancy. I am familiar with that thinking because I started my own marriage with the ER model. I changed my flawed thinking and am very grateful that is not the way I ended up.

Your feelings can make it challenging to resolve relationship conflicts and stick with your commitment to God and your spouse. However, your stubborn insistence to follow your own will rather than honour your commitment is a relationship breaker. If you want to be successful in a relationship, it takes commitment and there is no better way for you to get that commitment in your life than to follow and do exactly as God does in his relationship with us.

We serve a God of commitment.

God makes commitments to the people he loves. As we know, they are called covenants. He makes these solemn vows and these solemn promises to us. First he made them to the people of Israel and now to the rest of us. One of those covenants is known as the Palestinian Covenant. It was made by God to Jeremiah. He was a prophet and heard from God very clearly. He was just sitting around one day and heard the Lord speak to him.

> **This is the word that came to Jeremiah from the LORD. Listen to the terms of this covenant and tell them to the people of Judah and to those who live in Jerusalem. Tell them that this is what the LORD, the God of Israel, says:**
> Jeremiah 11:1-3

I want to be very clear and remind you that these next words are from God himself.

Aisle Seven | Your Lifetime Guarantee

> **Cursed is the one who does not obey the terms of this covenant.**
> Jeremiah 11:3

God says that the people will be cursed if they break the covenant he is making with them. God gives a fair warning about the consequences of breaking the covenant. To be cursed means to experience injury or hardship. It is better to obey rather than attract hardship.

A young man from the congregation was excited to tell me about his new relationship, a relationship he believed was blessed by God.

"We have such a wonderful relationship Pastor. You know we get along so well and we can communicate and we can share so deeply and we like the same things, and Jeremy, the sex is really good. The sex is great. And God is blessing us." he told me.

I stood flabbergasted in front of him. This misunderstanding, that God will bless disobedience, only creates more hardship. Believing that God will bestow blessings in your life, for your family, or your investments and work while you continue to violate his covenants of sexuality is simply not true. God does not bless disobedience of his will. The minute you willfully and knowingly step outside of the boundaries of his will you have placed yourself in a hostile world. It is like you have logged yourself online without any 'virus' protection.

You are spiritually and physically exposed, and your enemy is waiting for you.

When you are walking outside of God's plan for your life, good things might happen around you. Sometimes good stuff just happens, but that is not God blessing you. God said to Jeremiah in verse 3: **"cursed is one who does not obey the words of this covenant"**. If you take yourself outside of God's plan for your life, outside of what he said in the covenants and the promises he has given to you, and you know better, you are taking yourself outside of the realm of his blessings and that, my friends, is being cursed.

God continues his discourse with Jeremiah in verse 4: **"The terms I commanded your forefathers when I brought them out of Egypt, out of the iron-smelting furnace"**. In this verse, he is reminding Jeremiah that out of the heat and the oppression and the slavery they found themselves in, he made a covenant, a promise with them. He brought them out and he made some promises to them.

I said, 'Obey me and do everything I command you'
Jeremiah 11:4

Honestly, I sometimes have a hard time obeying God. Obedience is can be hard, but it is something you have to work towards because it will put you in the position where God can bless you. This is a commitment that you must keep. God wants you to commit your obedience to him, in your relationships, sexuality, dealing with your junk, thinking of other's needs and in all the different areas we looked at in the previous chapters. Then God makes this marvelous statement in verse 4: **"as you obey me, you will be my people"**, **a people that are called by my name, a chosen generation, a royal priesthood.** (1 peter 2:9) Not only does God make the bold assertion that they will be his people, he makes the covenant that: **"I will be your God"**. (Jeremiah 11:4)

Aisle Seven | Your Lifetime Guarantee

In the time of Jeremiah, the people were surrounded by other gods; gods of wood and stone, gods of mountains and gods in the water. During their walk to draw water from the well, they would pray that the god in the tree wouldn't attack them, and they would pray that the gods of the creatures would leave them alone so they could get there safely, and they would pray to the god in the well as they drew water, and then they would go back and they would make prayers and sacrifices. All of life was consumed by all these other gods. The Lord Jehovah says to his people, through Jeremiah, 'I will be your God, if you make a commitment to obey me'. Now, look what God promises to do as their God:

> **Then I will fulfill the oath I swore to your ancestors, to give them a land flowing with milk and honey - the land you possess today.**
> Jeremiah 11:5

God is very serious about our life with him.

God is serious about us living, as he has called us, to fulfill his covenant and his promises to us. God takes his commitments and covenants very seriously, but God knows that we cannot do it on our own. God knows that we will never fully obey everything that He asks us to do. Not one of us. If we cannot keep that commitment, then God cannot bless us. God loves us so much that he is not willing for that to happen; he does not want any of his people to be cursed, including you.

God uses the prophet Isaiah to tell his people about the One who is coming, whose name is going to be called Emmanuel (which means God is with us), and this is what he says:

The Relationship Depot

> **The Spirit of the Sovereign LORD is on me, because the LORD has anointed me to preach good news to the poor.**
> Isaiah 61:1a

Here is some good news for you: the poor he is talking about here bears no relationship to the money you have in the bank or invested in the stock market. Whether you are on some form of social assistance, or you just lost your job, or you are the wealthiest person in the city, the 'poor' in this verse relates to your ability to save yourself. You need to be fully obedient to Christ's commands, and keep his everlasting covenant. We are all poor. We have an inherent inability to obey God in our own strength. We have a poverty of spirit. (Matthew 5:3) What is this good news that he has come to preach? It is that Jesus Christ loves you and he has come so that you will have forgiveness of your sin; the bad things that you have done, the guilty feelings, the pain, hurt and the broken relationships that you have carried for so long. He has come to take away that pain and to restore you and make you new. He has come to preach good news to the poor.

There is more:

> **He has sent me to bind up the brokenhearted, to proclaim freedom for the captives and release from darkness for the prisoners.**
> Isaiah 61:1b

There have been dark times in my life; there have been painful times where I have been a prisoner to emotional pain, loss and heartache. There have also been times where I have been a prisoner to feelings of exaltation, joy and happiness that I did not find in God. Those feelings took me away from God. He has come to set us free from that as well. He says he has come:

> To proclaim the year of the LORD's favor and the day of vengeance of our God, to comfort all who mourn and provide for those who grieve in Zion— to bestow on them a crown of beauty instead of ashes, the oil of gladness instead of mourning, and a garment of praise instead of a spirit of despair.
> Isaiah 61:2-3

Look what God is committing himself to do for you, if you will obey. He has pledged to bind up your broken heart, to release you from darkness, from the distorted thinking of your own mind, and give light to your thinking.

We see Jesus, the anointed one, in the gospels casting out demons, healing the lame, giving the blind their eyes back. He made the paralyzed to get up and walk, brought back the dead and returned them to their families. God is committed to your healing.

God is also committed to your eternity.

> For God so loved the world that he gave his one and only Son, that whoever believes in him shall not perish but have eternal life.
> John 3:16

That is probably the most well-known verse of scripture, ever. But the next verse (17) says, **"For God did not send his Son into the world to condemn the world, but to save the world through him"**. He is committed to your eternity, not only in the world after death, but right here and now. He came to earth and demonstrated his commitment to you through his death, so that you can begin your eternity now. He is committed to you when you come in faith to him, and start walking in obedience with him. He is committed to you, from the moment that you were created, until all eternity. In our relationships we all have times of brokenness and pain. Through that hurt and pain God remains committed to us. You need to look at your own relationship and make a stronger commitment to it that reflects God's own commitment to you.

Matthew 3 talks about John the Baptist, who was Jesus' cousin. He was a little bit older and it was his job to let people know that Jesus was coming. In the King James Bible, John went out and preached: **"Repent for the Kingdom of God is at hand"**.

However, if you read in the Message Bible he says: **"Change your life, God's Kingdom is here! And then he was arrested"**.

Change your life. God's kingdom is here.

In Matthew 4, Jesus heard that John the Baptist had been arrested so he went to where John had been, and he picked up right where his cousin left off. He said, "Change your life, the Kingdom is here." Change your life, because I am here with you. I want to offer you the riches and the fullness and the most incredible experience, the greatest adventure you can ever be on. It is here, right now. I want you to make a commitment and walk with me. I want you to follow after what I say because this is the kingdom of God.

God offers you a lifetime warranty, eternal life; it is yours for the asking. That life is yours if you will make a vow of commitment to him. Reject all other forms of god in your life and worship Him alone. We, as the people of God, must become living proof of God's unchangeable guarantee of eternal life as we live in a covenant relationship of marriage with one another. It is time for Christians of all persuasions to 'shut the door' on divorce!

The act of divorce is a desecration of God's work of art. His art is bringing one man and one woman together until death. Nothing so perfectly represents who God is on earth as a marriage that is standing the test of time, the tides of change, and the disintegration of commitment in society. Churches in this great land are being torn apart by infidelity and unfaithfulness. The image of God is marred and bruised. The church, as the Body of Christ, is being ripped apart limb by limb as believers jump from relationship to relationship. I urge you to repent. I plead with you to keep your covenant relationship with your spouse. I implore that if you are not yet married, that you act in a pure and responsible manner sexually. When it is time for you to marry that you make an irrevocable covenant between your partner, God and his church.

God will not be mocked.
(Galatians 6:7)

We cannot go on living the lifestyle of the world and think that we will avoid the judgment of God. God is longing for his bride to be pure, precious, and holy. He promises that one day he will present her that way. To present her 'clean and radiant' means he will have to wash her of all filth. (Ephesians 5)

Build your relationship to Bible code

Romance	Build on RAYA love, to AHAVA love, and then bring in DOD love.
	Be courteously reverent to each other.
Courtship	Know God's word on marriage before making a commitment.
	Abstain from sexual sin.
Marriage	Seal the covenant with blood.
	Leave your parents and join with your new family.
	Go all out with your love, giving not getting.
Husband	Love yourself in loving your wife.
	Cherish your wife, like Jesus cherished the church.
	Lead like Christ in unselfish sacrifice.
	Your words should bring the best out in her.
Wife	Love your husband, support him and give him respect.
	Follow your husband's Christ-like, servant leadership.

Aisle Seven | Your Lifetime Guarantee

In 1876, George W. Robinson wrote the words to what would become my father's favourite hymn. My prayer is that these words touch your life, your pain, your plans, hopes, dreams, and your marriage. They are some of the finest words ever written on commitment that you will forever be able to say:

I am His, and He is mine.

Loved with everlasting love, led by grace that love to know;
Gracious Spirit from above, Thou hast taught me it is so!
O this full and perfect peace! O this transport all divine!
In a love which cannot cease, I am His, and He is mine.
In a love which cannot cease, I am His, and He is mine.

Heav'n above is softer blue, Earth around is sweeter green!
Something lives in every hue Christless eyes have never seen;
Birds with gladder songs o'erflow, flowers with deeper beauties shine,
Since I know, as now I know, I am His, and He is mine.
Since I know, as now I know, I am His, and He is mine.

Things that once were wild alarms cannot now disturb my rest;
Closed in everlasting arms, pillowed on the loving breast.
O to lie forever here, doubt and care and self resign,
While He whispers in my ear, I am His, and He is mine.
While He whispers in my ear, I am His, and He is mine.

His forever, only His; Who the Lord and me shall part?
Ah, with what a rest of bliss Christ can fill the loving heart!
Heav'n and earth may fade and flee, firstborn light in gloom decline;
But while God and I shall be, I am His, and He is mine.
But while God and I shall be, I am His, and He is mine.

The Relationship Depot

We are privileged to know and worship a covenant-keeping God. Follow Jesus Christ, as God asks of us. Make and keep your relationship commitments to God and your spouse for a lifetime.

THE RELATIONSHIP PRAYER

Dear God, my Father,

Thank you for your amazing love in my life. Thank you for caring for me and wanting the best for my life. It is my desire to honour you in my relationships. Your intention for my life is the best intention. There is no other purpose higher for me than what you have planned. I desire to be obedient to your plan so that my relationship can be a reflection of who you are: perfect, holy, complete and good.

Thank you, that you are a forgiving God. Through your Son Jesus Christ you have made a way for all my selfish, sinful attitudes and behaviors to be forgiven and forgotten. Thank you that you do not hold my past against me, but bring to my past reconciliation and restoration as I confess my wrongdoings that are contrary to your Holy Word.

Thank you for healing the hurts and wounds of my spirit that have been placed upon me by myself and others. I understand that your healing comes as I forgive. As I feel powerless to forgive, I humbly ask that you would forgive, through me, and that your love would be seen in my attitudes and actions, even towards those who I may consider my enemies.

Lord, I confess that my sexuality is your gift of intimacy to me. You created me as a sexual person to be a reflection of who you are. May my sexual behavior reflect this divine purpose. Give me the strength to use my sexuality only for the holy purpose you have created it for, and never to use my sexuality for my own selfish ends.

Lord, teach me to listen. Teach me to listen to you first, and then to the people you have placed in my life. Help me value what is important to them. Create in me a quiet mind that always seeks to understand another's point of view. Help me mature so that I can relax in the knowledge that you love me so completely that I do not need to seek the impossible from someone else. Help me rest in your Word which teaches me that you know all my needs and will supply all my needs, including my need for intimacy, safety, significance, and sexual wholeness.

Thank you Lord, for your covenant relationship with me, your commitment to my future, sealed in blood. Help me to patiently seek your will in the covenant relationship of marriage. When I feel like giving up, strengthen me by your Spirit so that I will know that I am doing your work, by making my marriage work. Remind me of the vows made in front of others, but before you; for better or worse, for richer or poorer, in sickness and in health, in joy and in sorrow, to love and to cherish and to be faithful to you alone, as long as we both shall live.

Thank you for the friendship and companionship that comes from you through others. Thank you for the promise of a love that is true and secure as you, God, are placed first in my life and in my relationship. To honour you with my life, and through my relationship, is to fulfill my greatest purpose.

February 14, 2011
Sudbury, Ontario, Canada

The Relationship Depot

Review

Saying you are committed is easy yet following through during challenging times tests your commitment. These are times that challenge you to grow. You become what you are committed to as illustrated by the Green Bay Packers fans who wear costumes to demonstrate their allegiance.

Our feelings can make it challenging to resolve relationship conflicts and stick with our commitment to God and our spouse. To be successful, it takes commitment. We serve a God of commitment.

Being clear about God not blessing what is actually disobedience. Yes obedience is hard to do, that is the first commitment you get to practice, between you and God.

Shut the door on divorce, instead grow and change your life to a commitment to God and your spouse.

Biblical Instructions

> **Tell them that this is what the LORD, the God of Israel, says: 'Cursed is the one who does not obey the terms of this covenant— the terms I commanded your ancestors when I brought them out of Egypt, out of the iron-smelting furnace.' I said, 'Obey me and do everything I command you, and you will be my people, and I will be your God. Then I will fulfill the oath I swore to your ancestors, to give them a land flowing with milk and honey'—the land you possess today."**
>
> **I answered, "Amen, LORD."**
>
> Jeremiah 11:3-5

For God so loved the world that he gave his one and only Son, that whoever believes in him shall not perish but have eternal life. For God did not send his Son into the world to condemn the world, but to save the world through him.

John 3:16-17

Building activities

1. To understand the degree of sincerity in God's command to obey his covenants, what is an example of God's work in a covenant you have undertaken?

2. What are some of the messages the world has told you about divorce that you might still hold?

3. Take three minutes to read the relationship prayer once a day. Hint, try to do it at the same time each day as this will help you develop the habit.

Acknowledgments

Heather Campbell, my writing partner extraordinaire, took on much more than she bargained for in attempting to turn a preacher into a writer.

Kate Pautler, who managed to edit my thoughts into coherence.

Tarra Batten-Johnson-Legault who is teaching me to pay attention to details.

Stephanie Palmer who helped start me on this whole adventure of writing.

The family of All Nations Church, Sudbury, Ontario, who have given me the privilege of sharing God's message with them most Sundays since 1978; To this family who listened and took the words of those sermons, with the help of the Holy Spirit, into their hearts and lives and who believe that the only faith worth having is an obedient faith lived out in our everyday lives, your encouragement to keep battling through life's trials is deeply appreciated.

My Pastor's Prayer Partners, who pray for me each week and during the delivery of each Sunday morning message; thank you for your faithfulness, diligence and courage.

Joshua Sklar, former Associate Pastor, All Nations Church and a supportive friend, for his contributions to the final chapter.

As the writer to the Ecclesiastes states there are "no new ideas under the sun". So, to all the writers and thinkers that I have read or heard, you all have had a part in the formulation of the ideas written in this book, and I thank you for 'going before'.

My mother Jean, who loves the Lord Jesus Christ first and loves her son, no matter what.

My wife, Eileen, for always believing that there was more to me than even I knew, and without whom there would be no relationship to write about.

The Lord Jesus Christ, who promised me through his word very early in my life that "what he had begun he would finish"; for not giving up on a relationally challenged rebellious young man. And HE is not finished with me yet! Just ask my wife.

HOW TO FIND MORE FROM JEREMY MAHOOD

You can experience Jeremy Mahood live Sunday mornings at 10am EST at www.allnationschurch.ca/live-stream

Forthcoming book:
THE CHARACTER OF CHRIST IN YOU
Developing spiritual maturity

www.jeremymahood.com